Spirit Freedom and Power

Spirit Freedom and Power

Changes in Pentecostal Spirituality

Angelo Ulisse Cettolin
Foreword by Rikk Watts

WIPF & STOCK · Eugene, Oregon

SPIRIT FREEDOM AND POWER
Changes in Pentecostal Spirituality

Copyright © 2016 Angelo Ulisse Cettolin. All rights reserved. Except for brief quotations in critical publications or reviews, no part of this book may be reproduced in any manner without prior written permission from the publisher. Write: Permissions, Wipf and Stock Publishers, 199 W. 8th Ave., Suite 3, Eugene, OR 97401.

Wipf & Stock
An Imprint of Wipf and Stock Publishers
199 W. 8th Ave., Suite 3
Eugene, OR 97401

www.wipfandstock.com

PAPERBACK ISBN: 978-1-4982-9373-0
HARDCOVER ISBN: 978-1-4982-9375-4
EBOOK ISBN: 978-1-4982-9374-7

Manufactured in the U.S.A.

All Scripture quotations, unless otherwise indicated, are taken from the Holy Bible, New International Version®, NIV®. Copyright ©1973, 1978, 1984, 2011 by Biblica, Inc.™ Used by permission of Zondervan. All rights reserved worldwide. www.zondervan.com The "NIV" and "New International Version" are trademarks registered in the United States Patent and Trademark Office by Biblica, Inc.™

Scripture quotations are taken from the Holy Bible, New Living Translation, copyright ©1996, 2004, 2007, 2013, 2015 by Tyndale House Foundation. Used by permission of Tyndale House Publishers, Inc., Carol Stream, Illinois 60188. All rights reserved.

This book is dedicated to my wife, Robbie, who has supported me in many ways through countless hours of both research and production. I also want to thank my family members, Joseph, Ursula, Jayson and Evangeline, for their good humor and encouragement.

Contents

Foreword by Rikk Watts | xi
Preface | xv
Acknowledgments | xvii
Introduction | xix
Abbreviations | xxiii

Chapter 1: What Do We Mean by Spirituality?

    Introduction | 1
    Historical Use of the Term | 2
    Catholic and Protestant Traditions | 4
    Contemporary Usage | 5
    The Influence of Secular Spirituality | 6
    Models of Christian Spirituality Today | 8
    Integration of Typologies | 9
    Common Features | 10
    The Process of Sanctification | 12
    Conclusion on Spirituality | 13

Chapter 2: Early Pentecostalism

    Three Waves | 15
    Historical Background | 16
    Classical Pentecostalism | 21
    Origins and Globalization | 21
    Early Australian Pentecostalism | 23
    The AoG and Its Spirituality | 29
    Conclusion on Early Pentecostal Spirituality | 30

Chapter 3: The Distinctiveness of Pentecostal Spirituality

Theological Distinctive | 32
Observations on Pentecostal Spirituality | 33
Primal Spirituality | 35
African-American Sources and Features | 35
Experience of God in Liturgies and Rituals | 36
Experiencing the Fullness of the Spirit | 39
Supernatural Experience of the Holy Spirit | 39
Implicit Values | 40
Passion for the Kingdom | 41
Glossolalia (Tongues-Speaking) | 41
Postscript on Postmodernism | 43
Classical and Current Pentecostal Spirituality | 45

Chapter 4: Contemporary Pentecostal Spirituality

Introduction | 47
Recent Developments | 47
Changes in Style and Structure | 53
New Networks | 55
Social and Political Involvement | 56
Worship Music | 57
A Fundamental Change | 57
Survey of Pastors | 58
Experiences and Practices | 58
Private Devotional Practices | 61
Church Services and Practices | 62
Community Service and Outreach | 64
Beliefs and Attitudes | 64
A Mixed Picture | 66

Chapter 5: Assessing the Results

Introduction | 67
Reflections of Key Ministers | 68
Changes in AoG (Pentecostal) Spirituality | 69
Conclusions | 71

CONTENTS

Chapter 6: Reflections

Sociological Insights | 72
Institutionalization | 73
Institutional Dilemmas | 75
Mixed Motivation | 76
Administrative Order | 78
Symbolic Dilemma | 78
Dilemma of Power | 81
Dangers of Delimitation | 82
Keeping the Dilemmas Viable | 83
Biblical Analysis | 84
Innovation and Routinization | 87
Theological Reflections | 89
Pentecostal Ecclesiology | 90
Trinitarian Ecclesiology | 92
A Community of the Spirit | 95
Trinitarian Pentecostalism | 96
Theology of Spirit Baptism | 99
Integration—Trinitarian Spirit Baptism | 101

Chapter 7: Conclusion

Change Is in the Air | 105
Spiritual Freedom and Flexible Structures | 108
A Call for Action | 111
Reform and Renewal | 113

Bibliography | 115

Foreword

THIS IS A TIMELY book. Pentecostalism has in my lifetime moved from its somewhat suspect origins on the margins of the Western working class to the center of global Christianity. It is now one of the world's most dynamic and thriving expressions of Christian faith. Along with its younger sibling—the Charismatic renewal movement—it comprises the second largest sector of the church (27%; 8% of the world's population) and by 2025 they are expected to almost double their share (44%; Pew, 2011). Lacking the long institutional history and cultural embeddedness of say the Roman or national churches, Pentecostalism's growing appeal across the entire range of cultural and societal landscapes—including the West, where Christianity is in many respects in decline—is impressive to say the least.

For Cettolin this is in part due to the Pentecostal preference for a dynamic experience of God's life-giving presence—his freedom and power—over the precise, fixed, and even rigid theological systems of more traditional forms of Christianity. As such it might reflect, at least in Western settings, a preference for a genuine, authentic, and creative "spirituality" over against what might otherwise be perceived as stultifying and impersonal, academic "religion." If so, it might be significant that it was precisely these kinds of dissatisfactions that led first-century pagans to abandon the impersonal and distant classical gods for the more relational deities of the Eastern mystery religions, including that other strange Eastern import: Christianity.

But this has not come without significant change, arising from and creating a series of challenging dilemmas (Cettolin's extensive chapter 6 is very informative on these matters). So, for example, in terms of his study of the Australian Assembles of God / ACC, many pastors continue to practice praying in tongues in their private devotions. But in collective worship there is a distinct movement away from individual expressions of tongues, interpretation, and prophesy, to more orchestrated and formally led corporate manifestations, with perhaps occasional short times of co-ordinated charismatic expression such as free worship and singing in the Spirit. Whatever the reasons—e.g., concern over misuse/abuse of gifts, logistical problems of various kinds arising in larger gatherings, a changing culture where such are not considered appropriate, or a preference for less risky and thus less stressful worship environments—this shift stands in tension with classical Pentecostalism's officially promoted doctrine of the individual experience of a baptism in the Holy Spirit, evidenced in tongue-speaking. There is, then, a growing gap between the official doctrine, with its emphasis on individual experience, and formal services that effectively promote the collective and the institutional.

This inevitably raises the question: Is this merely a sign of an inexorable creeping calcification that seems to afflict all renewal movements to some degree or another? Cettolin does not think so. Current Pentecostal spirituality still emphasizes the reality of freedom and power; only the forms—arising from a changing culture—and structures—which need to be there for any human institution to survive—are different. And these too can be seen as the work of the Spirit; after all, an essential characteristic of Pentecostalism is its flexible, adaptive, and innovative nature.

And here I think Cettolin has hit on something profound. It was Hellenism's emphasis on unchanging rational forms and the primacy of reasoned perfection that imprisoned the ancient world in eternally repetitive cycles with no possibility of change. It took Jerusalem's contrary view that creation's goodness was necessarily about the real possibility of genuine growth that opened the way to the modern world (so Edwin Judge, *Gospel Conversations* website). Similarly, Iain McGilchrist, *The Master and His Emissary*, has recently argued that while we surely need the left brain's single-minded focus, abstraction, precision, and clarity, its perfection comes at the cost of an empty, static lifelessness. Perhaps what Pentecostals have unwittingly anticipated and answered—perhaps through the leading of the Spirit?—is McGilchrist's impassioned plea for the needful primacy of the right brain with its emphasis on the personal, the particular, the implicit, with room for growth, change, and interconnection. Change, in the world God created, is to be expected.

Foreword

Now, as designers tell us, the more we move away from the Platonic delusion of a single perfect static ideal, the more the character of the designer comes into play. And perhaps this might say something to Pentecostals. Power and freedom are wonderful things. But unless they are guided by truly godly character they can soon be turned to demonic ends. There is a reason the Spirit points us to Christ. It is in Jesus that we see most clearly who God is, and that means, not just his power and freedom to do as he wills, but his character: his mercy, compassion, justice, self-sacrificial love, etc. The power and freedom of the Spirit, with all the possibility of change he brings, must be nurtured and expressed in the context of the fruit of the Spirit, and particularly in terms, not of ethics or virtue, but of trust (faith), hope, and care (love). And these, as Mark Strom has argued, are not merely a fundamental new morality, but an entirely new way of knowing. If this is indeed the case, then it might just be that the essential spirituality of Pentecostalism—the dynamic experience God's power and freedom—has caught something of what it means to be his designers in a world characterized by change.

Rikk Watts
Professor of New Testament
Regent College, 2016

Preface

While at times I have made critiques of the contemporary church, I love and am personally committed to the local church. I have a passion to see the church be all that God intends and gifted her to be. Finally, while much of the conversations in this book are about the Holy Spirit my goal is also to please my Father God and the Lord Jesus Christ. My prayer is that you, the reader, will be stirred to seek after all things of the Spirit that have been promised to us in Holy Scripture.

Acknowledgments

I WISH TO THANK MY academic colleagues and staff at Eastern College, Australia, who deserve special mention for their personal support, particularly Principal Dr. Cheryl McCallum, Dr. David Morgan, Rev. Cheryl Osment, Rev. Dr. Jeff Pugh, Dr. Tom Edwards, Dr. Art Wouters, Dr. Michelle Sanders, Steve Bradbury, Rika Mason, Ps. Glenn Tweedie, Dr. Andrew Schmidt, Neil Horvath, Sue Grechko, Sarah Michaels, Aaron Garth, and Rohan Edmeades. I also wish to thank my colleagues at Harvest Bible College for their encouragement, particularly Dr. Brendan Roach, Dr. Jon Newton, Dr. Ian Grant, Dr. Phillip Hughes, and Grant Buchanan.

Introduction

The Pentecostal movement in the Christian church emerged at the turn of the twentieth century emphasizing the need for believers to have an authentic and powerful *experience* of the Holy Spirit—this was evidenced by speaking in tongues (or glossolalia). It passionately advocated the return to a pristine early Christianity in which empowerment by the Spirit was seen as essential and part of the normal Christian life. More recently, however, some Pentecostal and Charismatic movements are playing down features of historic or classical Pentecostalism and moving toward more traditional or mainline expressions of the Christian life in their practices and beliefs.

Sociologists have proposed that as organizations, such as churches, develop they tend to become more structured, moving away from spontaneity toward more order and routine. Tensions begin to develop between the institution and "charismatic" freedom.[1] It seems that in the Western world pressures from growing institutionalization and modernity is leading to a change in the spirituality of Pentecostal leaders and their churches.

I went on a search to discover whether this was really the situation in my own context, and if so what the ramifications might be.[2] My concern was for Pentecostals to retain their radical edge, being faithful to their historic

---

1. Weber, *Theory of Social and Economic Organization*, 400, 439–40.

2. The author's doctoral research was on the changing nature of Pentecostal spirituality. It involved a survey of lead pastors in the Assemblies of God in Australia, also known as Australian Christian Churches (AoG/ACC). The study sought to understand what was emerging in the Pentecostal spirituality of its pastors. The theory that needed investigating was whether "growing institutionalization was changing the pastors' Pentecostal spirituality."

Introduction

roots, and yet still develop a mature and relevant spirituality for this present day and age. Is it possible for pastors and leaders to have ringing in their ears the sounds of early Pentecostalism, while still interfacing with the changing context of a complex postmodern cultural milieu in the twenty-first century? Could there also be any lessons here for all Christians, of whatever persuasion, about their current spiritual practices? While today's Pentecostal spirituality is certainly shaped by classical early Pentecostal expressions, did it need to develop in some way to remain dynamic and vibrant?

To answer these questions the nature of Pentecostal spirituality needed to be uncovered. Scholars have acknowledged a distinctive Pentecostal or Charismatic spirituality, but there was no consistency in defining its characteristic features. The term "Pentecostal/Charismatic" is often used synonymously. The view adopted here is that the classical Pentecostal movement is based in the revival at the turn of the twentieth century and the neo-Pentecostal or Charismatic (renewal) movement is of the second half of the twentieth century— two waves within the one larger movement. Pentecostal churches can represent both.[3] Of particular importance to them is a crisis-type "second blessing" experience after conversion, often referred to as "the baptism in the Holy Spirit," which is evidenced by speaking in tongues. From the 1960s until recent times, the term "Charismatic" was used of those who held to the same "second blessing" experience but generally chose to remain within their non-Pentecostal churches. Since the 1980s, evangelicals of the "Third Wave" movement, while they do not classify themselves as either Pentecostal or Charismatic, hold to the validity of the gifts of the Spirit but do not require a climactic second blessing experience evidenced by speaking in tongues. More recently, the term "Charismatic" or "Neo-Pentecostal" has been used to describe those that hold to the validity and use of the gifts of the Spirit for today but do not mandate the requirement of speaking in tongues to validate their experience of the Spirit. All four streams have influenced Pentecostal churches and ministers including the Assemblies of God in Australia, also known as Australian Christian Churches (AoG/ACC), and proponents of all the approaches are represented within these churches.

In chapter 1, we will explore what Christians mean by "spirituality" in general and in comparison with the more secular use of this term. For Christians, "spirituality" is more than just a human quest or journey. It is

---

3. At times I use the generic term "Pentecostal" as inclusive of both, while at other times I use "Pentecostal/Charismatic" to include both. The term "Pentecostal" is commonly used to refer to those who are committed to traditional or classical Pentecostal beliefs and practices.

Introduction

an attraction to things of the Spirit and the conscious living of a Christian way of life empowered by the Holy Spirit. Pentecostal spirituality, as one form of Christian spirituality, particularly emphasizes God's Spirit working in the process of sanctification and empowerment for ministry. However, the essential nature of Pentecostal/Charismatic spirituality is wider than what is described in Pentecostal theology and this required some empirical observation and analysis.

In chapter 2, the origins and developments of Pentecostalism are outlined and what particularly distinguished the Pentecostal understanding of the Christian life. Various views are surveyed in chapter 3 to distill the essential features of Pentecostal spirituality. Remarkably there is considerable consistency despite the varied global phenomena. At the heart of the diverse Pentecostal spiritualities there is a shared *experience* of the Holy Spirit and a *practice* of the spiritual gifts that unifies this global diversity.

In chapter 4 a summary of my research findings about some contemporary expressions of Pentecostal spirituality are explained.[4] Although the Pentecostal experience is still important for Pentecostal leaders it appears there have been changes in certain practices and beliefs, particularly concerning Spirit baptism and speaking in tongues.

In chapter 5 views of various Pentecostal ministers are interacted with and some personal observations are made about the direction that Pentecostalism is heading, particularly in the Western world. My reflections in chapter 6 result in a call being made for the adoption of a distinct Pentecostal church structure (ecclesiology) that has a clear Trinitarian perspective. Some suggestions are also made for Pentecostals and Charismatics to expand their theological understanding of "baptism in the Holy Spirit."

The seventh chapter seeks to draw some final conclusions. An essential aspect of Pentecostal spirituality is its inherent flexibility and its adaptive, innovative nature. Despite some humble origins the Pentecostal movement is now reaching the middle class in the Western world. Although there are some tensions over charismatic freedom, an organizational structure appears to be developing that is facilitating not only the movement's preservation but also its significant ongoing growth. With this in view a number of suggestions around the practices and beliefs (spirituality) of Pentecostalism are made.

4. The results of a national survey of AoG/ACC senior pastors plus interviews with its key leaders and also my personal observations over many years as a Pentecostal minister showed there is support for the hypothesis that the spirituality of Pentecostals was changing.

Abbreviations

ACC Australian Christian Churches

AG Assemblies of God (USA)

AoG Assemblies of God (Australia)

NLT New Living Testament

NIV New International Version

1

What Do We Mean by "Spirituality"?

Introduction

AN EMPIRICAL STUDY INTO "spirituality" is initially confronted with the question of how to define the term. It may be the most ambiguous term in our time:

> For those in the Church, some take the term for granted, some rigidly define it, and others seldom give it a thought. In broader circles, spirituality has come to mean an urge or power within us that drives us toward meaning for our lives.[1]

The English term "spirituality" may have been originally coined by Roman Catholic theologians to refer to a mystical relationship with God, but it is now commonly used to refer to a whole range of approaches existing in different branches of the church that allow a more personal and life-transforming relationship with the God that is revealed in Jesus Christ through the work of the Holy Spirit. In earlier centuries, Christians often used words like "devotion" or "piety," but now these terms have developed a "flavor of other-worldly sentimentality."[2] In contrast, the term "spirituality" does not have the same connotation but is more inclusive of everyday life. Often the term is used to refer to levels of personal "spirituality." People compare or measure themselves as being more or less spiritual than others and judge other people's spiritual performance and state.[3]

---

1. Hagberg and Geulich, *Critical Journey*, 2.
2. Holt, *Brief History of Christian Spirituality*, 16.
3. The author's doctoral research did not seek to measure spirituality per se, or any

Historical Use of the Term

In classical Greek thinking the philosophers saw all living things as possessing spirit (*pneuma*—the breath of life) and as having a soul or life principle (*psyche*). The soul was believed to be immaterial and to survive the death of the material body. Spirituality was the basis for human attributes of thought, language and rationality; it defined humanity.[4]

For Christians, on the other hand, the term "spirituality" leads first to a reflection on the person and work of the Spirit of God. It finds its root in the word "spirit," which in biblical usage can refer to both the human spirit and the divine Holy Spirit. In the Old Testament, the word for "spirit" in Hebrew is *ruach*,[5] and in New Testament Greek, *pneuma*.[6] In ancient Israel as in ancient Greece, humans are considered to have the "breath of life" (*ruach/spirit*). However, the Old Testament provides another dimension of meaning because Israel's God actually transcends the material world, which is his creation. The "Spirit of the Lord" (*ruach elohim*) is a manifestation of God's power and wisdom.[7] In the New Testament, although there is no direct Greek equivalent of the word "spirituality," the Holy Spirit is often referred to as the transforming presence of God in the life of a believer.

> Now, the Lord is the Spirit, and wherever the Spirit of the Lord is, he gives freedom. And all of us have had that veil removed so that we can be mirrors that brightly reflect the glory of the Lord. And as the Spirit of the Lord works within us, we become more and more like him and reflect his glory even more. (2 Cor 3:16–18 NLT)

It is right to speak of "*Christian* spirituality" as the term was in fact first used among Christians. Paul declares that the Holy Spirit assists us in our prayers and intercessions (Rom 8:26–27) and produces the qualities of a Spirit-controlled life (Gal 5:22–23). Paul also speaks of believers as *spiritual* or *pneumatikos* (1 Cor 2:13–15; 3:1; Gal 6:1). He makes the contrast with unbelievers whom he calls the *psychikos*, those without the Spirit.[8] For New Testament exegete Gordon Fee, the evidence is

---

individual's discrete expression of spirituality but rather to gather and measure information about Pentecostal spirituality in pastors that can be observed and measured.

4. Kleinknecht, "Pneuma in the Greek World," 334–59.
5. Baumgärtel, "Spirit in the OT," 359–68.
6. Kleinknecht, "Pneuma in the Greek World," 332–59.
7. Singleton et al., "Spirituality in Adolescence," 3.
8. Schweitzer, "Pneuma, Pneumatikos in O.T.," 436–37.

What Do We Mean by "Spirituality"?

overwhelming that Paul, quite in keeping with first-century usage, never intended *pneumatikos* to refer either to the human spirit or to some vague idea like "spiritual," which in English serves as an adjective meaning "religious," "nonmaterial," "spooky," "nonsecular," or "godly." In every instance in Paul its primary referent is the Holy Spirit, even when contrasted with "material blessings" in 1 Corinthians 9:11.[9]

Fee goes on to clarify that God's aim in our lives is "spiritual" in the sense that redeemed by the death of Christ, we might be empowered by his Spirit both "to will and do for the sake of his good pleasure." True spirituality is nothing more or less than life in the Spirit:

> One is spiritual to the degree that one lives in and walks by the Spirit; in Scripture the word has no other meaning, and no other measurement.... When Paul says to the Corinthians (14:27), "if any of you thinks he or she is spiritual," he means, "if any of you think of yourselves as a Spirit person, a person living the life of the Spirit." And when he says to the Galatians (6:1) that "those who are spiritual should restore one who has been overtaken in a transgression," he is not referring to some special or elitist group in the church, but to the rest of the believing community, who both began their life in the Spirit and come to completion by the same Spirit.[10]

The failure to recognize the central role of spirituality in Paul has stemmed, in part, from the use of the lowercase English word "spiritual" to translate the adjective *pneumatikos* in the Pauline letters. For Paul this word is primarily an adjective for the Spirit, referring to that which belongs to or pertains to the Spirit. To be "spiritual" from Paul's point of view is to be a Spirit person, whose whole life is full of, and lived out by, the power of the Spirit.[11]

For Paul, the Christian life is by definition a "spiritual" life in the sense that it is a life of prayer and devotion, of rejoicing, thanksgiving and petition (1 Thess 5:16; Acts 16:25; 1 Thess 3:9–10; Phil 1:3–4; Col 1:9–11). Fee points out 1 Corinthians 14:1–19 "gives clear evidence for the fact that praying in the Spirit, in tongues, held a significant place in Paul's own prayer life." He considers four texts (1 Cor 14:2, 14–17, 18–19; Rom 8:26–27) and

---

9. Fee, *Paul, the Spirit, and the People of God*, x.
10. Fee, *Listening to the Spirit in the Text*, 5–6.
11. Ibid., 33–39.

concludes that all together they indicate Pauline "spirituality" included, as an integral part, prayer that was Spirit-inspired and Spirit-uttered. "This is not the only form of prayer for Paul, but one more indication that for him, 'spirituality,' even in our sense of that term, was primarily 'Spirit-uality.'"[12] This contrasts markedly with today's common usage of the term as referring to merely a human quest.

The New Testament's unique understanding of "Charisma" within the above framework of "Spirit-uality" is crucial, particularly when considering sociology's perspective, where generally the human dimension of the term "charisma" is in mind. Max Weber and other sociologists emphasize the residence of "charisma" as "extraordinary powers" or "magical powers" in the *human* charismatic leader.[13] The New Testament on the other hand, sees the "charismata" as being available to both leaders *and* followers and puts the emphasis on their *divine* origin and empowerment. Sociology refers to natural human qualities, whereas the New Testament refers to supernatural grace gifts of the Spirit of God. While helpful insights can be drawn from sociology, the New Testament understanding's of the charismata as a divine quality, in contrast to the reference to extraordinary human qualities, is of central concern here.

Catholic and Protestant Traditions

The word "spirituality" was first used in the fifth century to speak of the renewing touch of the Holy Spirit in the life of a Christian.[14] The term seems to have been first popularized in French Catholic circles by Catholic theologians using it to refer to a mystical union with God. By the seventeenth century it came to mean the conscious living of a Christian way of life, especially as it relates to the interior dimension in contrast to the outward form, rituals and institutions.[15] It emerged as a well-defined branch of theology in the eighteenth century when Giovanni Scaramelli (1687–1752) of the Society of Jesus established ascetical and mystical theology as a science of the spiritual life.[16] These became specialized fields that described the teachings of the mystics and the ordinary Christian disciplines. In the

---

12. Ibid., 39–47.
13. Weber, *Theory of Social and Economic Organization*, 362, 439–40.
14 Giles, "Quest for Spirituality?," 1.
15. Singleton et al., "Spirituality in Adolescence," 3.
16. Ferguson et al., *New Dictionary of Theology*, 656–57.

twentieth century these two subdisciplines combined into one: "Spiritual theology" or "Spirituality."[17]

For many Protestant writers, the term "spirituality" has a biblical connotation to it. The Puritan John Owen (1616–1683) used the term in the seventeenth century to refer to the sphere over which the Holy Spirit has influence. The word was also used by the nineteenth-century Scottish evangelist Henry Drummond who spoke of "spirituality" as that which the Holy Spirit produces in the life of the believer.[18]

Contemporary Usage

Today many Roman Catholics and liberal Protestants use the term to describe the religious person's quest to find a deeper relationship with God. In this framework it is often assumed that religious persons are involved in the same human quest whatever their persuasion: Christian, Buddhist, Muslim and so forth. While not denying that religious people of various persuasions often embark on a similar human quest for meaning in their search for the Divine, Evangelical Christians (including Pentecostals and Charismatics), generally use the term "spirituality" to refer to the work of the divine Spirit of God in a person's life. This understanding of spirituality involves a relationship between the whole person and a holy God who reveals himself through both testaments and ultimately in the person of his unique Son, Jesus Christ. This relationship, broken by sin, can only be restored through faith in Jesus Christ. The goal of Christian spirituality is conformity of a person's heart and life to the character of Jesus as Lord (1 Cor 12:3). The assurance of Christian spirituality is the presence and power of the Holy Spirit in the life of the believer, resulting in conformity to God's revealed will.[19]

In everyday usage the term "spirituality" often refers to the *human* search for meaning. Although an ill-defined and ambiguous term, it is popular. For many people, "religion" refers to an established system and institutions, whereas "spirituality" implies personal participation and is less tied to the connotation of institutional constraints. Despite the term "spirituality" having a long history of Christian usage some conservative Christians are wary of using the term, arguing that it reflects New Age

17. Holt, *Brief History of Christian Spirituality*, 17.
18. Giles, "Quest for Spirituality?," 1.
19. Ferguson et al., *New Dictionary of Theology*, 656–57.

thinking. However, it is not important that the term is not found in the Bible. As a well-known word, it can assist us to come to an understanding about the Holy Spirit, who is the basis of a spirituality that is established in the revelation of God given in Jesus Christ.[20]

The Influence of Secular Spirituality

Now in postmodern societies, the term "spirituality" still retains the sense of a person's interior life but is beginning to be understood as no longer necessarily linked to institutional religion, sometimes even standing in opposition to it.[21] In a broad and secular sense "spirituality" has been defined as a yearning for self-transcendence and our response to this longing. It is the human search for identity, meaning, significance and purpose. In its widest sense it can refer to any religious or ethical value that is from which one's actions flow. There are spiritualities related to all religions and many pursuits arising in the human spirit.[22]

In the Western world many people are looking to make sense of life and to experience something more than what a material existence has to offer but they do not think it is necessary to believe in God or go to church in order to have a spiritual life. This quest is commonly called "spirituality." This trend toward secular spirituality has been helped by the fact that "spirituality" has no single, clear, unambiguous meaning. Many people do not want to be religious but that does not mean that they do not want to be spiritual—but often it is spirituality on their own terms.[23]

Another important factor is that Western societies have moved from being traditional to post-traditional since the end of the Second World War[24] and a major change in religion has occurred globally since the 1960s, particularly in Anglo-Celtic societies. This is often reflected in a change of church attendance patterns. In advanced industrial societies attendance is in general decline with shifts from weekly to monthly or holiday attendance. Sociologists have attributed this trend to a variety of factors including, boredom during services, lack of motivation, generational incompatibility

---

20. Giles, "Quest for Spirituality?," 1.
21. Singleton et al., "Spirituality in Adolescence," 3.
22. Toon, *What Is Spirituality*, 14–16.
23. Edgar, "Spirituality," 14.
24. Giddens, *Beyond Left and Right*, cited in Hughes, "Spirituality," 6.

of belief and social changes brought about by modernity.[25] Research across sixty-five different countries indicates that out of twenty advanced industrial countries, sixteen demonstrate a declining rate of monthly church attendance.[26]

In the United States of America a 2009 Gallup poll found that church attendance among Protestants has remained stable at roughly 45% since 1955, while attendance among Catholics has dropped from 75% to 45%, although it has remained stable since 1995 despite the negative press of abuse scandals.[27]

The position in the United States of America is ambiguous due to criticism of conventional surveys. Gallup's self-reporting telephone survey indicates a lower 37% of Americans report that they attend church weekly or near weekly in 2013.[28] However, online surveys indicate substantially lower attendance rates.[29] Furthermore, methods that do not rely on self-reporting estimate even lower rates. A 2005 study found that just 22% of Americans attend services weekly. Hadaway and Marler claim this further gives evidence that Americans tend to overreport worship participation and are less religiously active than the polls might show.[30]

In Australia, church attendance fell by 7% in participating denominations in the National Church Life Survey, 1996–2001(NCLS). Contrary to these trends, since the 1960s, Pentecostal churches in Australia have been increasing, but the NCLS reveals significant movement, with 38% transferring in from other denominations or no recent church, 15% moving out to other denominations, and 17% moving out to no church at all.[31]

Religion used to be more a community affair, now increasingly in the developed world *individuals* make the decision as to what they will believe, how they will relate to God, join a church and move on. During this time of change, Pentecostal churches have been more accommodating for the individual. Harvey Cox says that "speaking in tongues" was "radically democratizing."[32] Today the market conscious individual, as consumer,

25. Bellamy et al., *Why People Don't Go to Church*, 253–69.
26. Inglehart and Baker, "Modernization, Cultural Change," 19–51.
27. Lydia Saad, "Churchgoing among US Catholics."
28. Gallup, "Religion: Gallup Historical Trends."
29. Grossman, "Poll: Americans Stretch the Truth."
30. Hadaway and Marler, "How Many Americans."
31. Bellamy and Powell, "2001 Church Attendance Estimates," 15.
32. Cox, *Fire from Heaven*, 95.

evaluates a church's sense of community, its worship, and beliefs. This individualism is also evidenced in the number of people who fail to identify with any religious community and in the growth of the neo-pagan and new age movements.[33] This reality needs to be engaged by the church if it is to reach people in a post-Christendom world.

Models of Christian Spirituality Today

Due to the extensive number of views on Christian spirituality, a number of models or typologies have been constructed to help us understand the phenomena. Graeme Chapman identifies seven theological models and assesses their relative strengths and weaknesses: evangelical, liturgical, activist, contemplative, relational, charismatic and ecumenical.[34] Kevin Giles adds two more: liberal and sacramental.[35] Others could be added: holiness, missionary, social justice, mercy and feminist.

On the other hand, attempts have been made to categorize Christian spirituality into broader classifications. Peter Adam argues for three groupings. First, the Reformed and Evangelical view is that all God's saving words and works are found within the Bible and within that period of revelation of the Old and New Testaments. In the second group Roman Catholics, Eastern Orthodox and some Pentecostals and Charismatics are positioned together, as those who hold to the view that in addition to the Bible, God has continued to do saving works and speak his words to the church. Third, is the Quaker and Liberal view that revelation comes directly from God today by observation, reason, experience and emotion. The second and third views allow for an ongoing work of the Spirit in new contemporary revelations for hearing God speak today.[36]

General categorizations such as these are problematic, as they tend to overstate what these groups represent. The majority of Pentecostals and Charismatics would hold that prophecies or revelations subsequent to the canonical Scriptures are not to be considered on the same level of authority as the Bible. Further, many Evangelicals believe that God is still speaking to

---

33. Hughes, *Spirituality as an Individual Project*, 1–10. More evidence about the growing individualism of religious practice is provided by the *Australian Community Survey* (1997–98) conducted by NCLS Research and Edith Cowan University.

34. Chapman, "Theology, Spirituality and Ministry," 1–3.

35. Giles, "Quest for Spirituality," 1–3.

36. Adam, *Hearing God's Words*, 40–41.

his church in the world today. Concerns that the authority of church leaders could become primary over Scripture or that a pneumacentric view of Christianity downgrades Christology and the value of Scripture, are not inevitably the case. It is possible to hold both—to the primacy of the authority of Scripture and also that the Spirit of God who inspired the human authors of Scripture continues to communicate and reveal himself today. A similar evaluative process for interpretation and application of Scripture should be able to be employed to assess any professed revelations from God.

As will be seen in chapter 2, reawakening the value of experiencing the immanent in the Spirit of God has been Pentecostalism's great contribution to the church. There is always an ongoing danger that in the process of encouraging people to experience God, we may lose our grasp on understanding God. However, most Pentecostals and Charismatics have a high view of Scripture that requires any experience to always be grounded in biblical truth.[37] Care does need to be taken in interpreting experiences,[38] but there is an equal danger that we can become so preoccupied with propositional truth that we miss out on the Person our theological propositions point to. There does not need to be a dichotomy between experience and truth—truth is more than simply accurate information. A number of scriptures refer to the testimony that Jesus himself actually was the truth and that he came to bear witness to the truth (Matt 22:16; Mark 12:14; John 1:14, 17; 14:6; 18:37). As Chant says, "Truth is a Person long before it is objective data."[39]

Integration of Typologies

While Pentecostal/Charismatic spirituality emphasizes the work and initiative of the Holy Spirit,[40] openness to different traditions make us aware of our own parochialism and ethnocentrism and helps us appreciate the variety of approaches to Christian spirituality. Awareness of the various forms

---

37. Middlemass, *Interpreting Charismatic Experience*, 193.

38. Klein et al., *Introduction to Biblical Interpretation*, 149–50, suggest a number of tests to validate creative interpretations of Scripture that may similarly be useful to evaluate charismatic phenomena.

39. Chant, editorial, 1–2.

40. Holt, *Brief History of Christian Spirituality*, 18–21.

and styles of spirituality can help preclude an insular vision limited to one's own tradition.[41]

Ben Johnson makes a compelling plea for an incarnational spirituality that draws upon other types and combines them into a creative whole. He advocates an integrated model that recognizes the importance of the biblical norms of an evangelical piety and also the freedom of the Spirit as in charismatic piety. This approach values the sacramental aspect of life and engages with the real needs of people, as in activist piety. To develop the intellect is as valid as retreats for self-denial and self-examination.[42]

Brian Edgar agrees that "spirituality" is an integrative concept that should bring together, and not set against each other, different aspects of life—the intellectual and devotional, experience and doctrine, reflection and action, the physical and spiritual, community life and solitude, celebration and sacrifice. Fragmentation or internal conflict may be an indication that one's spirituality needs attention.[43]

Common Features

Despite the considerable variety of forms displayed in the Christian tradition, there are still certain norms of genuine spirituality and there are boundaries and limitations. These are found primarily in the Scriptures and also the early church creeds. There are a number of common underlying themes and features of genuine Christian spirituality:

First, it is not an optional extra as though some people are "spiritual" and others are not. It is how people express their faith in one way or another. All the various forms of "spirituality" deal with a person's relationship with God, and as such are very "personal," although this does not mean private or individualistic.[44] "Spirituality" has simply become the contemporary word of choice for expressing how we live with God in this world.[45]

Second, it is more than a mode or type of relating to God and it refers to the working of the Holy Spirit within believers to make them more like Christ (2 Cor 3:18). For Christians, "spirituality" is the sphere in which the Holy Spirit has direct influence. The suffix "-ity" expresses a state or

---

41. Ferguson et al., *New Dictionary of Theology*, 657.
42. Johnson, *Pastoral Spirituality*, 74–75.
43. Edgar, "Spirituality," 15.
44. Ibid.
45. Thompson, *Soul Feast*, 6–7.

condition of being spiritual, of being indwelt and guided by the Holy Spirit.[46] It is the encounter of the self with God and one's personal response to the God who calls.[47] It is based in the love and grace of God rather than human ability. Talents and capacities are important but the initiative and emphasis lies with God (Eph 2:8).[48]

Third, it is focused on the triune God, who is Father, Son and Holy Spirit. Something is a Christian exercise because of the *content* rather than the *method*. The key issue is the intention or the focus involved, rather than simply the technique.[49] "Spirituality" involves the human response but is always guided by the Spirit to the revelation of God in Jesus Christ.[50]

Fourth, "spirituality" finds its characteristics from the Christian belief that humans are capable of entering a relationship with a God who is both transcendent as well as indwelling the human heart. However, this self-transcendence is a gift of the Spirit who establishes a life-giving relationship with God in Christ within a believing community.[51]

Fifth, the term "spirituality" also relates to its outworking in the way one behaves and relates to the external world. It is about how Christians follow the Holy Spirit's guidance and how they respond to his action upon their spirit.[52] It is not simply for the "interior life," but as much for the body as for the soul, and is directed to the implementation of both the commandments of Christ to love God and our neighbor.[53]

A robust spirituality will also be connected to ethics. Mulholland therefore defines spiritual formation as "a process of being conformed to the image of Christ for the sake of others."[54] It does not refer to just a privatized experience but it involves the whole of life.

Sixth, a helpful working definition of spirituality in the Christian context is that of a "lived experience," one that actualizes a fundamental

---

46. Toon, *What Is Spirituality*, 13.
47. Johnson, *Pastoral Spirituality*, 46, 65.
48. Edgar, "Spirituality," 15.
49. Ibid.
50. Toon, *What Is Spirituality*, 17.
51. Sheldrake, *Spirituality and History*, 52–53.
52. Toon, *What Is Spirituality*, 17.
53. Wakefield, *Dictionary of Christian Spirituality*, 361–62.
54. Mulholland, *Invitation to a Journey*, 12.

dimension of being human, the spiritual dimension.[55] As Paul the apostle said, "If we live by the Spirit, let us also walk in the Spirit" (Gal 5:25).

Finally, Russell Spittler characterizes "spirituality" as referring to the cluster of acts and sentiments that are informed by the beliefs and values of a specific religious community. "Liturgy" describes what people *do* when assembled for worship and "theology" defines systematized and usually *written* reflections on religious experience. By contrast, it has been argued, "spirituality" focuses on people's pietistic *habits*. The elasticity of the term comes from the wide variety in which worshippers express themselves.[56] However, these particular definitions are too restrictive as liturgical acts and theological beliefs are actually helpful in measuring various expressions of spirituality. It will be seen that in Pentecostal spirituality, as in a number of other traditions, there is in fact a close connection between liturgy, theology and spirituality.

The Process of Sanctification

Although for Pentecostals the contemporary term "spirituality" generally relates to the experience of the empowerment of the Spirit, the Reformed view of Christianity finds its connections are with an older theological term, "sanctification." In post Reformation theology, justification refers to the instantaneous work of God alone, in justifying the sinner. Sanctification, refers to the ongoing work of God in the believer, in which the believer is called to cooperate. In "sanctification" the goal is to become more holy or Christ-like. In using the word "spirituality" the emphasis falls on the work of the Spirit in this process. The Reformers made a distinction between justification and sanctification. They regarded the former as a legal act of divine grace affecting the judicial status of humanity and the latter as a moral, spiritual and re-creative work, changing the inner nature of believers. Though in no way confusing justification and sanctification, in order to avoid the danger of works-righteousness, the Reformers preserved the closest possible connection between the former, in which the free and forgiving grace of God is strongly emphasized, and the latter, which calls for the cooperation of the believer.

Berkhof says of Pietism and Methodism (precursors to Pentecostalism), that great emphasis was placed on constant fellowship with Christ as

---

55. Albrecht, *Rites in the Spirit*, 23.
56. Spittler, "Spirituality, Pentecostal and Charismatic," 1096.

means of sanctification. As observed in the next chapter, the early Holiness Pentecostals like the Methodists often so emphasized sanctification that justification was eclipsed. The result was they did not always avoid the danger of self-righteousness and legalism. Wesley did not merely distinguish justification and sanctification, he virtually separated them, and spoke of entire sanctification as a second gift of grace, following justification by faith. Although he spoke of sanctification as a process, he also held that the believer should pray and seek out full sanctification at once by a separate act of God.[57] Similar problems emerged in classical Pentecostalism, as will be seen in the next chapter.

Later, influenced by Rationalism and the moralism of Kant, sanctification ceased to be regarded as a supernatural work of the Holy Spirit and was reduced to the level of mere moral improvement by natural human powers.[58]

In the New Testament, the word for sanctification is *hagiasmos* (Rom 6:19, 22; 1 Cor 1:30; 1 Thess 4:3, 4, 7; 2 Thess 2:13; 1 Tim 2:15; Heb 12:4; 1 Pet 1:2) and the word *hagios* is used in connection with the Spirit of God nearly a hundred times. Sanctification takes place in the believer's life partly as an immediate operation of the Holy Spirit, and also by the use of certain "means of grace" such as the exercise of faith, the study of God's Word, prayer and association with other believers—all features that form part of "spirituality." The Bible does not just urge moral improvement for its own sake, but moral improvement in relation to God, for him and for his service. It insists on sanctification and is essentially a supernatural work of the Spirit of God in the life of the believer. It is never merely a natural process in the spiritual development of people or mere human achievement, as is spoken of in much of modern liberal theology. It is a work of God in which believers cooperate. God is the author not the believer (2 Cor 7:1; Col 3:5–14; 1 Pet 1:29).[59]

Conclusion on Spirituality

"Christian spirituality" implies more than simply a universal human religious experience or quest—it is a descriptive term for the work of the Holy Spirit. It is the attraction to things of the Spirit rather than earthly

---

57. Berkhof, *Systematic Theology*, 530–31.
58. Ibid., 531.
59. Ibid., 528–35.

things and the conscious living of a Christian way of life. It mainly relates to the interior dimension but cannot be separated from its outworking in the external world. Although "spirituality" is a descriptive term of the process and working of the doctrine of sanctification, it also has a wider scope. One of the important insights offered by the study of spirituality comes from observing its interaction between doctrine, discipline (as in authority), corporate worship and the whole lifestyle of the believer. Together, these four factors provide the basic pattern for understanding spirituality. Although doctrinal theology, particularly of sanctification, both forms and informs spirituality, equally spirituality gives shape and substance to theology. As will be seen in chapters 2 and 3, the Pentecostals' theology on "the second blessing" has impacted their spirituality. However, Pentecostal spirituality has also impacted Pentecostal theology.

The next chapter introduces the historical background to Pentecostalism as a context to understand Pentecostal spirituality, which shares in a basic Christian experience. Many of its aims, values and features are not in themselves unusual and apply to other Christian traditions as well. Pentecostal/Charismatic characteristics have appeared before in the history of Christian spirituality through the ages.[60] However, what is unique is that the combination of characteristics is new.[61] Pentecostal/Charismatic spirituality does bring a unique emphasis on the initiative and work of the Spirit in the believer. The next chapter sets the background to understand the interaction between Pentecostal beliefs and behavior in the context of theology and culture as we endeavor to understand the resulting pattern of Pentecostal spirituality.[62]

---

60. Albrecht, *Rites in the Spirit*, 23.
61. Burgess et al., *Dictionary of Pentecostal and Charismatic Movements*, 5.
62. Ferguson et al., *New Dictionary of Theology*, 657.

2

Early Pentecostalism

Three Waves

UNDERSTANDING THE HISTORICAL BACKGROUND of Pentecostals and their theology of the Spirit helps to inform the nature of their spirituality.[1] The emergence of three waves of the Pentecostal movement, "classical" Pentecostalism, the "Charismatic" movement, and mainstream church renewal or "Third Wave," has had worldwide impact.[2] In the 1960s and 1970s, the neo-Pentecostal or Charismatic movement led many mainline church Christians to the same experiences as classical Pentecostalism.[3]

Over the years, classical Pentecostals generally came to recognize spiritual gifts in members of the so-called "mainline" or "historic" denominations. Some "Charismatics" remained in their "historic" denominations. Some formed new churches and others transferred into and influenced the classical Pentecostal assemblies.

Charismatics did not necessarily accept all the doctrines or all the proscribed activities of the classical Pentecostals but they adopted various Pentecostal spiritual practices, including speaking in tongues, prophecy, healing ministry and aspects of Pentecostal-styled praise and worship. With the rise of "nondenominational" Charismatic churches a decade later, the term "Charismatic" was widened to refer to all groups outside denominational Pentecostalism where spiritual gifts are exercised. It is now often

---

1. Anderson, *Introduction to Pentecostalism*, 9–15, 190–92.
2. Burgess et al., *Dictionary of Pentecostal and Charismatic Movements*, 1–6.
3. Holt, *Brief History of Christian Spirituality*, 14.

impossible to distinguish between Pentecostals and Charismatics. There are often as many liturgical and theological differences between classical Pentecostals as there are between them and Charismatic churches.[4]

It appears that the influence of "Charismatics" and "Third Wavers" from the mainline denominations has had considerable influence on both the development of theology and spirituality in the Pentecostal movements. In the transition and development of Pentecostalism some argue that as a result its pastors have lost something of their early emphasis on the experience and dynamic of the Spirit.

Both early and contemporary Pentecostal spirituality and its practices cannot be understood without discussion of classical Pentecostalism's historical background. In the beginning of this chapter the context is set for our exploration of early or classic Pentecostal spirituality, which is dealt with later.

Historical Background

Many scholars are convinced that the charismata or "spiritual gifts" are found in all ages but usually at the margins of the established church.[5] Certainly spiritual gifts appeared in the radical edges of Protestantism and were almost always regarded as sectarian movements. During the Reformation, the gifts of the Spirit were virtually unknown, except for reports in the discredited Anabaptists. Later, the Quakers, founded by George Fox, (1624–90) emphasized "Inner Light" through the Holy Spirit and various manifestations of the Spirit's work was evident. John Wesley, founder of Methodism, countered a critic who said glossolalia had ceased, by favorably referring to the Cévenol revivalists in France. During the nineteenth century, the charismata increased, especially in the Methodist and Holiness movements. There were many reports of revivals with speaking in tongues and other charismata including: the preaching of Edward Irving (1792–1834) in Glasgow and London; in the Catholic Apostolic Church, until 1879; Sweden in 1841; the Johann Blumhardt (1805–80) "healing home" in Germany; North American Shakers from Russia and Armenia in 1855 who migrated to America from 1900–1910, forming Pentecostal churches that

---

4. Anderson, *Introduction to Pentecostalism*, 144–62.

5. See Anderson on the reports of charismata associated with Pentecostalism, which are common throughout two thousand years of Christianity, in *Introduction to Pentecostalism*, 19–23.

predated the Pentecostal denominations. Various revival movements at the turn of the twentieth century created an expectancy and longing for revival in many parts of the world.[6]

A widely held view is that Pentecostalism was consciously founded as a reenactment of early Christianity—the experience of the early church appeared to be such a contrast to formal and powerless twentieth-century churches.[7] This position claims that the Pentecostal movement began in the United States, although deriving much of its theology and practices from the earlier British perfectionistic and revivalist movements, notably the Holiness movement, the Catholic Apostolic movement of Edward Irving, and the British Keswick "Higher Life" movement.

Edward Irving unsuccessfully attempted restoration of the New Testament charisms, although tongues and prophecies were experienced in his Regent Square Presbyterian Church in 1831. His followers failed to restore the "five-fold ministries" referred to in Ephesians chapter 4 but Irving identified glossolalia as the standing sign of the baptism of the Spirit, a major plank of Pentecostal theology.[8] The Keswick "Higher Life" movement thrived in England after 1875. Its teachers changed the content of the second blessing from the Wesleyan emphasis of "heart purity" to "enduement of power for service." It has been argued that the Holiness Movement and the Keswick Convention continued John Wesley's teaching of entire sanctification when the Methodist churches had lost interest in it. Wesley had been influenced by the Pietist movement of the seventeenth and eighteenth centuries that stressed the personal experience of God and spawned the Moravian movement of Count von Zinzendorf (1700–60).

Many were longing for "something more" than the justification by grace they had experienced at conversion. They lacked the power to live the expected new life of holiness, avoiding the pleasures of the world and being committed to evangelism and social reform. What was new in Pentecostalism was identifying Wesley's "second blessing" with the biblical "baptism in/with the Holy Spirit." The outward sign of this baptism was speaking in tongues followed by the "spiritual gifts" listed by Paul in 1 Corinthians.[9]

6. See Allan Anderson's account in *Introduction to Pentecostalism*, 23–24, 38.

7. This was not the first or last attempt to rediscover the power of the early church. The restorationist movement of the nineteenth century in America led the Disciples of Christ and the Churches of Christ to try and get free of denominationalism and return to a form of early Christian worship.

8. Synan, "Origins of the Pentecostal Movement," 2.

9. Holt, *Brief History of Christian Spirituality*, 124–25.

Vinson Synan concurs that by the time of the Pentecostal outbreak in 1901 in North America, there had been a century of movements emphasizing a second blessing called the "baptism in the Holy Spirit." During the nineteenth century, many Methodists claimed to receive this experience, which brought spiritual power and cleansing, but no one saw any connection with speaking in tongues.[10]

This doctrine had a significant influence on Pentecostalism. Anderson says Wesley's doctrine of entire sanctification and the possibility of spiritual experience subsequent to conversion "undoubtedly constituted the egg that hatched the Holiness movement and its offspring, Pentecostalism."[11] It is arguable that the first Pentecostal churches in North America came out of the Holiness movement prior to 1901 and kept most of their perfectionistic teaching and practices. These included the mainly African American Church of God in Christ (1897), the Pentecostal Holiness Church (1898), Church of God (Cleveland, Tennessee), and other small groups. These churches formed as "second blessing" Holiness denominations and simply added the baptism in the Holy Spirit with glossolalia as "initial evidence" of a "third blessing." Synan says, "It would not be an overstatement to say that Pentecostalism, at least in America, was born in a holiness cradle."[12]

Historical writings usually trace Pentecostal origins in North America to a revival started on January 1, 1901, at Bethel Bible School in Topeka, Kansas, run by Charles Parham (1873–1929), a Holiness teacher and former Methodist pastor.[13] There is, however, no consensus as to Pentecostalism's origins. Others propose that it began with the African American William J. Seymour (1870–1922) and the Apostolic Faith Mission in Los Angeles. However, there are a significant number who say their members spoke in tongues before either Seymour or Parham. A fourth view is that it is sovereign work of God with no leader or group but a spontaneous and simultaneous global work of the Spirit.[14]

Parham subsequently developed the "evidential tongues" doctrine that became the hallmark of classical Pentecostals.[15] He also taught that "tongues" was a supernatural impartation of human languages (*xenolalia*)

---

10. Synan, "Origins of the Pentecostal Movement," 2–3.
11. Anderson, *Introduction to Pentecostalism*, 25–27.
12. Synan, "Origins of the Pentecostal Movement," 5.
13. Hollenweger, "Pentecostals and the Charismatic Movement," 550.
14. Kärkkäinen, *Pneumatology*, 87–88.
15. Blumhofer, *Restoring the Faith*, 56.

to miraculously evangelize the world in the end times.[16] For Parham, it was essential to embrace three distinct crisis experiences: salvation, sanctification and baptism in the Holy Spirit with the evidence of speaking in known or unknown foreign languages.

Parham was eventually rejected as the founding father of Pentecostalism by almost the entire North American Pentecostal movement, many of whom subsequently formed the Assemblies of God (AG). They could not justify on biblical grounds the idea of sanctification as a second definite work of grace whereby the sinful nature was eradicated—many had simply not experienced a crisis of sanctification. They therefore assumed that this was not a precondition for receiving either the baptism in the Spirit or to speak in tongues. Second, they rejected the view that tongues always had to be in a known foreign language.[17] However, despite differences during the first decade, the Pentecostal movement showed remarkable tolerance to a variety of theological opinions.[18]

The pivotal moment in the development of this new style of Christian spirituality was in a storefront church on Azusa Street in Los Angeles in 1906. The remarkable African American Holiness preacher William Seymour introduced both black and white seekers to the "baptism with the Holy Spirit" and speaking in tongues.

Seymour preached in a time of racial tension. A descendant of slaves, he had to listen to Parham's lectures through an opened door sitting outside his Bible class. Hollenweger says what was extraordinary about Seymour was his *spirituality* enabling him to endure persecution from Christians, non-Christians and white Pentecostals without become embittered. For him, Pentecost was more than speaking in tongues—it was overcoming hate by love and living differently to the prevailing culture.[19] This revival was a fusion of white American Holiness religion with worship styles derived from the African American Christian tradition which had developed since the days of chattel slavery in the American South.

> The admixture of tongues and other charisms with black music and worship styles created a new and indigenous form of Pentecostalism that was to prove extremely attractive to disinherited

16. Synan, *Origins of the Pentecostal Movement*, 6.
17. Anderson, *Introduction to Pentecostalism*, 34–35.
18. Roebuck "Emerging Magisterium?," 173–76.
19. Hollenweger, "Pentecostals and the Charismatic Movement," 550–51.

and deprived people, both in America and other nations of the world.[20]

Hollenweger, believes the developing Pentecostal spirituality was generally despised because of its lowly black origins. The revolutionary nature of the spirituality where whites and blacks, clerics and workers, men and women worshipped together as equals was misunderstood.[21] The attitude and values of the time were captured by Frank Bartleman, a white Azusa participant who exclaimed that "the color line was washed away in the blood." People were represented from all the ethnic minorities of Los Angeles, a city he called "the American Jerusalem."[22]

This was a predominantly black church with black leadership, rooted in the African American culture of the nineteenth century.[23]

Hollenweger says the founder of Pentecostalism could be either Parham or Seymour, depending on whether the essence of Pentecostalism is in either a specific doctrine of a particular experience (speaking in tongues) or else in its oral, missionary nature and ability to break down barriers, as in Azusa Street. Hollenweger's choice of Seymour is not on historical sequence (Parham was earlier), but on theological principles—the basis on which the Pentecostal message spread around the world.[24] From these humble beginnings news of this "outpouring" of the Holy Spirit spread to the world. For over three years the Apostolic Faith Mission conducted three services a day, seven days a week, where thousands received the tongues baptism. News of the revival was spread through the *Apostolic Faith*, a paper sent free of charge to some fifty thousand subscribers. People began to receive the tongues experience without going to Azusa Street and many traveled the world to spark other Pentecostal movements. The first wave of missionaries produced the classical Pentecostal movement consisting of eleven thousand denominations.[25]

---

20. Synan, *Origins of the Pentecostal Movement*, 6.
21. Hollenweger, "Pentecostals and the Charismatic Movement," 550–51.
22. Synan, *Origins of the Pentecostal Movement*, 6.
23. Anderson, *Introduction to Pentecostalism*, 43–44.
24. Hollenweger, "Black Roots of Pentecostalism," 42–43.
25. Kärkkäinen, *Pneumatology*, 87.

Classical Pentecostalism

William H. Durham led many people into the Pentecostal movement. His "Finished Work" theology of "progressive sanctification" led to the formation of the Assemblies of God (AG) in 1914.[26] It was not long before a movement that started as a reaction against dogma and creeds became engaged in doctrinal wrangling. By 1916, Pentecostalism was doctrinally divided into three competing groups: "Second Work" (Holiness) Trinitarians, "Finished Work" (Baptist) Trinitarians and "Finished Work" Oneness Pentecostals, divisions that all still remain. Other divisions were on the authority of spoken prophecy, diverse eschatological interpretations, church government, personality conflicts and racial differences. Today, "Finished Work" Trinitarian Pentecostalism is the major expression of the movement and is the position taken by the major classical Pentecostal denominations, (including the AoG/ACC). In North America, Pentecostals were often despised and rejected by the established churches because they were thought to be mostly poor, uneducated people. Pentecostals in turn charged the "historic" churches as having lost the power of the Holy Spirit. Despite this, the movement expanded rapidly because of its exhilarating and spontaneous spirituality. This development was not like the dissemination of some new idea but more "like the spread of a salubrious contagion."[27]

Origins and Globalization

Although the origins of Pentecostalism are recent, it must be recognized that the experiences that gave it birth lie deep within Christian history.[28] The Wesleyan influence gave Pentecostals an understanding of the importance of heart religion and crisis experience in the Christian life. The Holiness connection brought a concern for the abolition of slavery, women's rights, prohibition and reform of society.[29] In North America, Pentecostals received the enthusiastic, corporeal worship style from African American believers.[30]

---

26. Synan, *Origins of the Pentecostal Movement*, 6–7. By 1993, the AG had over two million members in the US and 25 million adherents in 150 nations.
27. Cox, *Fire from Heaven*, 71.
28. Leech, *Soul Friend*, 151.
29. Land, *Pentecostal Spirituality*, 480, 492.
30. Kärkkäinen, *Pneumatology*, 87.

It is often assumed that Pentecostalism had its origins in North America, however, scholars more recently acknowledge that it had several beginnings. Everett Wilson argues that many subsequent "outpourings" indicate no claim can be made to exclusivity. "There was no containing these diffused outbreaks of fervor or of demonstrating in respect to sequence and causality the relationship between them."[31] A study of Pentecostalism need not focus exclusively on North America since non-Western groups have developed their own "analogous, cognate forms . . . but in a variety of settings." If they have similar or identical Pentecostal features, "it is notable that they have never had more than the most tenuous ties to the North American institutions."[32] It must be noted that one of the challenges in understanding Pentecostal spirituality is that most of the relevant literature is from North America and Europe which limits our global perspective on Pentecostal spirituality.

Historians who take a global perspective have challenged the view that Pentecostalism was birthed in North America, and subsequently imported to others places, such as Europe, Asia, and Australia. This view sees the world as increasingly becoming one single connected place. During the late nineteenth and early twentieth centuries physical movement and communication became quicker and almost instantaneous.[33] The phenomenon of globalization can be defined as "the compression of the world and the intensification of consciousness of the world as a whole."[34] The globalization thesis posits that our "social communication links are worldwide and increasingly dense." As a result people, cultures, and social groups "previously more or less isolated from one another are now in regular almost unavoidable contact."[35] With regard to Pentecostalism, David Martin provides an insightful explanation:

> Somewhere in the successive and increasingly unsponsored mobilizations of *laissez-faire* lay religion, running to and fro between Britain and North America . . . there emerged a many-centred mobilization . . . a potent variant capable of stomping alongside modernization world-wide.[36]

31. Wilson, "They Crossed the Red Sea," 91.
32. Ibid., 109.
33. Wolffe, *Global Religious Movements*, 1.
34. Robertson, *Globalization*, 8.
35. Beyer, *Religion and Globalisation*, 1–2.
36. Martin, *Pentecostalism*, 4–5.

Martin argues that the way faith works creates a mobilization from the bottom up by "unlearned and ignorant men." As a result the "fissiparous star-burst that follows" leads to many rival movements. This means "it does not make much sense to regard Pentecostalism as an imported package, especially in situations—the vast majority—which are replete with multicultural transfers." Rather it is a number of religious explorations that are "apt for adaptation in a myriad indigenous contexts."[37]

> Contemporary global dissemination means that whatever the initial effervescence in Los Angeles at the beginning of "the American century" the movement of Pentecostalism is multi-centred, and the spiritual contagion spreads. . . . Indigenization and autonomy are essential.[38]

Early Australian Pentecostalism

In Australia the development and growth of the Pentecostal movement is instructive. It began less than a decade after the earliest reported US incidents of the phenomenon, "certainly before any substantial institutionalization occurred" and, earlier than the formation of the larger denominations.[39] In his dissertation, "Spirit of Pentecost: Origins and Development of the Pentecostal Movement in Australia 1870–1939," Barry Chant makes some important findings. From its very beginning he claims, the Australian Pentecostal movement differed from its overseas counterparts.

It was primarily a middle class movement, not one of the disenfranchised, with its origins among people of relatively comfortable economic status. Chant convincingly makes the case that "deprivation theories" have proven inadequate to explain the origins and character of Pentecostalism in Australia and its distinctive doctrine and practice of the baptism of the Holy Spirit.[40] Second, Pentecostalism's beginnings were more rural than urban in comparison to the United States or Great Britain. Third, the first Pentecostal church was pioneered and pastored by a woman, Sarah Jane Lancaster and over half of the congregations by 1930, were established and led by women. Fourth, it was both a cosmopolitan and indigenous movement.

---

37. Ibid., 169–70.
38. Ibid.
39. Wilson, "They Crossed the Red Sea," 109–10.
40. Chant, *Spirit of Pentecost*, 541.

"Although it is commonly believed that Australian Pentecostalism was an American import, like Mormonism or the Jehovah's Witness movement, in fact, its roots were primarily European."[41] Although it benefited from overseas influences, the leadership and the major work were carried out by Australians. However, although news and ministry from other countries had an effect, the first Pentecostal meetings were not planned outreaches from overseas organizations but were "basically indigenous movements." Once the movement was underway, visitors from America, England and other nations helped to "shape the movement but not to make it."[42]

There was American input (Aimee McPherson, A. C. Valdez, Kelso Glover, Mina Brawner) over the first four decades but there were also significant contributions from other nations such as England, India, Scotland, South Africa and Wales. From the outset leadership was in the hands of Australians. Sarah Jane Lancaster, the founder and pastor of the first Pentecostal congregation, was Australian born, as were the founders of the second and third congregations. Other Australia-born early Pentecostal leaders included C. L. Greenwood, Philip Duncan, Charles and Will Enticknap, Joy Heath, Robert Horne, and many others.[43]

The first Pentecostal believers may have been influenced from overseas but their experience was their own. There was no three-stage initiation as Parham or Seymour had. Regeneration was for salvation; baptism in the Spirit was for service—evidenced by speaking in tongues. An early Pentecostal publication the *Good News Hall Statement of Faith* declared a belief that a definite physical manifestation accompanies the reception of the Holy Spirit. *The AoG Statement of Faith* was also clear about belief in the Baptism of the Holy Spirit for all believers with the initial evidence of speaking in other tongues.[44]

Chant's examination of the available evidence shows the movement did not start in a vacuum but in a seedbed of revivalism and the cosmopolitan nature of Australian Pentecostalism, has been evident from the

---

41. Ibid., 38–39.
42. Ibid., 204–5.
43. Chant, *Spirit of Pentecost*, 38–41, 543, and *Heart of Fire*, 24.
44. Article 5:13, *United Constitution of the AoG National General Conference*: "The Baptism in the Holy Spirit: We believe that the baptism in the Holy Spirit is the bestowing of the believer with power to be an effective witness for Christ. This experience is distinct from, and subsequent to, the new birth; is received by faith, and is accompanied by the manifestation of speaking in tongues as the Spirit gives utterance, as the initial evidence—Luke 24:49; Acts 1:4, 5, 8; 2:1–4; 8:15–19; 11:14–17; 19:1–7."

beginning.[45] He traces its origins from three major nineteenth-century tributaries; the Wesleyan movement, with its emphasis on entire sanctification; the ministry of John Alexander Dowie, with its focus on divine healing and separation from the world; and the Evangelical movement, with its fervent and growing desire for revival. He concludes that the early Pentecostal movement in Australia was in the main theologically Evangelical:

> What set it apart was the emphasis on the baptism of the Holy Spirit accompanied by speaking with tongues. Even acceptance of the gifts was not exclusively Pentecostal. There were many in the mainline churches who believed in divine healing. It was glossolalia that was the sticking point. . . . By insisting on the sign of tongues, they made it mandatory for people to have an experiential encounter with God.[46]

Chant's second major thesis is that Pentecostalism's main contribution to Australian Christianity has been an understanding that religious experience is vital to authentic faith. Although stirring of the affections has often been part of Christian expression, in Pentecostalism's teaching and practice, "such a personal perception and knowledge of God has been enshrined as an integral and ongoing element of Christian life." Study of its first few decades clearly demonstrates that "for most people, the perceived attraction of Pentecostal worship has been its focus on an experiential and sensate encounter with God."[47] There was more to Pentecostal spirituality than glossolalia. "Having experienced tongues, Pentecostals were inevitably open to other kinds of 'manifestations' . . . spiritual gifts such as prophesying and healing were encouraged. So, too, were phenomena such as tears, visions and physical trembling." At times, worship was extravagant and there were differences over what was acceptable. "However, one experience was never questioned and that was being baptised in the Spirit."[48]

Pentecostal manifestations had occurred, not without controversy, at early twentieth-century Keswick Convention meetings. Glossalalia and healings were reported in the Keswick Convention meetings of 1910 at Eltham in Victoria.[49] People even claimed to have received "the baptism of the Holy Spirit" with manifestations of glossolalia, before 1901.

45. Ibid., 205, 543.
46. Ibid., 543–44.
47. Ibid., 444–45.
48 Ibid.
49. Chant, *Heart of Fire*, 32.

The first Pentecostal assembly in Australia was the Good News Hall (1909–1935), located in North Melbourne, and was founded by a woman, Sara Jane Lancaster. It identified with the Dowie-Keswick tradition of holiness and set the pattern for early Pentecostals. The Hall's monthly publication, *Good News*, edited by Lancaster, frequently referred to visions experienced by attendees and claims of miraculous healings. This was the earliest Pentecostal paper in Australia[50] and it also referred to a group in Portland, Victoria, who claimed to have been baptized in the Spirit and spoken in tongues back in 1870.[51]

In 1926, *Good News* listed nine separate "manifestations" (along with Scripture references): "falling on the face; sighing; lifting up the hands; shaking, trembling, quaking; extraordinary manifestations; laying on hands; overcome as by wine; travail; and praying all night." The Hall often held up to twelve prayer meetings weekly, including "tarry meetings" to help people receive the baptism in the Holy Spirit. Prayer for the sick, "laying on of hands," "anointing with oil" and stories of healing by expelling demons was common. In line with their Holiness influence, association with the world was eschewed. A dust storm in 1926 was interpreted as a sign of God's impending judgment. There was concern over serious sins of murder, theft and adultery, but also cards, the theatre, dance and other worldly pursuits.

Sanctification was often seen in legalistic terms of absence of cosmetics and jewelry.[52] However, the Hall was also known for its more positive and practical endeavors, such as printing of literature, tract distribution, prayer for the sick and needy, "laying on of hands" for the baptism in the Spirit, and sponsoring of evangelistic campaigns. The Good News Hall flourished until the 1930s. Hostility due to doctrinal errors and female leadership never abated, but the Hall succeeded in planting churches in every state. "It was the original vine from which many . . . Pentecostal branches drew their early life."[53]

The Hall also responded to the social needs in Australia at a time, when, according to Chant, Pentecostalism usually focused on preaching, praying and evangelism. During the Great Depression in 1931, between 140 and 180 unemployed men came daily to the Hall to receive "both material

50. Lancaster, ed., *Good News* (1910) 3–5.
51. Chant, *Heart of Fire*, 43.
52. Ibid.
53. Ibid., 56, 120.

and spiritual food." On average every week, seven hundred free lunches and free clothing were given away. Another two Pentecostal groups began soon after Good News Hall. Keswick supporter Robert Horne started Southern Evangelical Mission (SEM). In 1916, Sunshine Gospel Hall became the third Pentecostal meeting place in Melbourne. From this revival, a church was organized and bought a theater at Bridge Road Richmond. In 1927 C. L. Greenwood became the pastor of "Richmond Temple" (AOG) until 1968. It became the Pentecostal center of Melbourne.[54]

The *Good News* publications of 1910–1934 refer to frequent experiences of holy laughter, singing in the Spirit, people falling prostrate, speaking in tongues, people overcome or "drunk in the Spirit," shakings, visions, healings and claims of xenolalia (speaking in foreign known languages). Chant gives chapter 15 in his thesis to a detailed analysis of accounts from a number of articles, reports and early teachings, mainly from *Good News*. The primacy of the experiential in early Pentecostalism through being baptized in the Holy Spirit and consequently speaking in tongues is clear. It was usual but not mandatory for people to be baptized in the Spirit at a "tarry meeting," based on Luke 24.49 as the proof text. It was common at Good News Hall to devote the Christmas holiday break to the priority of this type of meeting.[55]

Speaking in tongues was to become the point of demarcation between Pentecostalism and other previous revival movements that were also marked by various emotional phenomena, but none had enshrined such experiences in a biblical doctrine before.[56]

The available evidence suggests that all the various Pentecostal churches during the 1930s displayed a common position when it came to holiness, patterns of worship, the inspiration of the Bible and education. A spontaneous lack of ceremony was a feature of Pentecostal worship; vocal prayer, utterances in tongues, prophecies, testimonies, lively preaching and singing, laying on of hands for healing, baptism by immersion and use of the Authorized Version of the Bible, were all normally in evidence. The phenomenon of people collapsing "under the power of God" or "in the presence of God" occurred in Pentecostal meetings regularly over the years. In the Keswick tradition they subscribed to separation from the world; "the

---

54. Ibid., 48–51, 96–97.
55. Chant, *Spirit of Pentecost*, 497–538.
56. Ibid., 503–38.

theatre, the dance-hall, the fiction library—all were shunned."[57] Important was the conviction that glossolalia was the distinctive sign of the Spirit's coming and was divine in origin and therefore was more durable and valuable than ecstatic phenomena:

> Every experience was secondary to the one great experience of being baptised in the Spirit. No matter how intense or exciting or fulfilling it might be, only the infilling of the Spirit accompanied by glossolalia was ultimately acceptable. Tongue speaking was not an option. Everyone who was truly baptised in the Spirit was expected to do it.... It was a phenomenon which every believer was expected to experience.... The evidence indicates that most believers did.[58]

It is not possible decades later to know what percentage of people did in fact speak in tongues. Chant's own observation after forty years in ministry is that it was almost universal among Pentecostals in the 1950s and 1960s and that it would be reasonable to assume that this was the case in the 1920s and 1930s.

Today the AoG/ACC still requires pastors to speak in tongues before ordination. However, whether this requirement is still an important part of the spiritual life and experience of AoG/ACC pastors and their congregation will be examined later. Chant believes that despite Pentecostalism following the inexorable pattern of institutionalization, the emphasis on religious experience still remains dominant.[59] Many of Chant's findings on early Pentecostalism were also informative of early AoG (Pentecostal) spirituality.

Paul Grant, an AoG minister who was converted in 1938 and began full-time ministry in 1947, recalls early Pentecostal churches as "vigorous and pragmatic." He says they claimed an historic evangelical faith but "expressed it in ways that were lively." Sometimes they were confrontational and coercive. "Street or open air" meetings were a "regular part of the weekly church program." Although organized into denominational groups, many refused to refer to themselves as a "denomination." Many maintained weekly "tarry meetings" where the focus was on waiting on God for the

---

57. Chant, *Heart of Fire*, 141–143.
58. Chant, *Spirit of Pentecost*, 523.
59. Ibid., 523–24.

baptism with the Spirit and receiving of the gifts of the Spirit.[60] Grant describes the "order of service" in church services:

> Pentecostals expected "the leading of the Spirit" . . . at any service there would be joys and drama and spontaneous responses to the Spirit's promptings. Gifts of the Spirit, periods of worship and praise, testimonies, Scripture readings, an anointed song, a span of silent wonder, an exhortation, a sermon, prayer for special needs . . . these and other components helped to make up liturgies that fascinated and fed the people, informed and instructed the congregations, in the way of the "Spirit-filled life" . . . there was an expectancy that the unexpected, the surprising and the spontaneous would occur.[61]

The AoG and Its Spirituality

The Assemblies of God in Australia website states it is unable to trace its origins to any single leader, it does however, acknowledge that a number of early Pentecostal leaders were involved in its formation in the initial years in Australia, including Sarah Lancaster, A. C. Valdez, Smith Wigglesworth, C. L. Greenwood and P. B. Duncan. However, it says none were individually responsible for the AoG's formation:

> The Assemblies of God in Australia was formed in 1937 and has experienced consistent growth. It adopted a new name of Australian Christian Churches in 2007 and currently consists of over 1,000 churches with over 280,000 constituents, making it the largest Pentecostal movement in Australia.[62]

Chant's thesis (1999) relates to the first four decades of the Pentecostal movement before the *official* national formation of the Assemblies of God in Australia (AoG) in 1937. It would be fair to surmise that Chant's description of Pentecostal spirituality during the 1920s and 1930s reflects much of what early Pentecostal spirituality would have looked like. The first assemblies had actually already begun almost twenty years earlier and the official formation with less than forty congregations actually brought

---

60. Grant, *What Does It Mean*, 38–40.
61. Ibid., 44–45.
62. Assemblies of God website, "About Us," http://www.acc.org.au/about-us.

together three state-based Pentecostal movements (Assemblies of God in Queensland, Pentecostal Church of Australia in NSW and in Victoria).[63]

Early copies of the *Australian Evangel* claim it was the official organ of the Pentecostal Church of Australia in fellowship with the AoG in Britain, the United States, Canada and New Zealand.[64] Begun in July 1927, it mainly carried sermons from meetings in the Richmond Temple and news reports from the assemblies. It served members as a monthly magazine with sermons, reports, testimonies and advertisements.[65] The *Australian Evangel*, the publication of the Assemblies of God in Queensland (AGQ), and the *Glad Tidings Messenger*, the publication of the Pentecostal Church of Australia, were merged in 1937 and adopted a combined name, and later became known as the *Australian Evangel*. In 1997, this official AoG publication was renamed the *Evangel Now!* later changed into simply *Now!* This has now morphed into the *ACC EMag*, a quarterly electronic publication for ACC leaders.

A survey of the publications of the *Australian Evangel* from 1927–1938 reveals information consistent with the accounts given by Chant. There are regular articles, testimonies and reports from the Assemblies on divine healing, holiness, tongues as the evidence of the baptism in the Holy Spirit, visions, the gift of the Holy Spirit, seeking and tarrying for the Holy Spirit, falling under the power of the Spirit, deliverance from affliction of demons, deliverance from tobacco, the foursquare gospel including Jesus as Baptizer, the full blessing of Pentecost, being filled with the Holy Spirit, gifts of the Spirit including faith, healing, miracles, word of knowledge, word of wisdom, singing in the Spirit, Pentecostal Baptism, Holiness and Sanctification through the Spirit and revival.[66]

Conclusion on Early Pentecostal Spirituality

From the available literature early AoG (Pentecostal) spirituality is consistent with early Pentecostal spirituality in general, and closely reflects it. This information is supplemented by examination of the accounts of Pentecostal ministers interviewed to assist us in developing a more complete picture. Although there has been an increase in sociological research in recent

---

63. *Assemblies of God* website, 1, and see, *Australian Evangel*, November, 1942, 16.
64. Chant, *Spirit of Pentecost*, 125.
65. Chant, *Heart of Fire*, 96, 234.
66. See *Australian Evangel / Glad Tidings Messenger*, 1927–1938.

years, such as Christian Research Association and the National Church Life Survey, there has been virtually none for the early years of the Pentecostal movement.[67]

Pentecostal ministers who provided reflections on their early spirituality confirm the data from the historical literature—*experience* was clearly emphasized. One AoG minister interviewed in 2004 and over sixty years of age commented that a feature of early Pentecostalism was a belief in "experience over theology" and a radical encounter with the baptism of the Holy Spirit. Another minister in the same age group (60–70 years) confirmed there was clearly an emphasis on the baptism of the Spirit. Speaking in tongues as "the evidence" was regarded as "an emphatic teaching," he said. Yet another minister in his late seventies emphasized that "holiness was a significant distinctive of early Pentecostalism." He also offered that "tongues speaking would be seen, heard and known in an authentic Pentecostal church"—as it was an early "Pentecostal distinctive."

In the next chapter the views of a number scholars and commentators on the distinctive features of Pentecostal theology and practice mainly in regard to Spirit baptism and the characteristics of early Pentecostal spirituality will be further explored. The influences of Pentecostalism in North America and Europe were relevant to our study of early Australian Pentecostalism, whether this is viewed from the perspective of the theory of the globalization of religion or on the "importation" model.

---

67. Chant, *Spirit of Pentecost*, 82. This made the accumulation and interpretation of quantitative data on Pentecostal spirituality in the early years difficult. However, qualitative data from interviews was also relied on.

3

The Distinctiveness of Pentecostal Spirituality

Theological Distinctive

ALTHOUGH THERE ARE THREE contemporary waves that are commonly spoken of as characterizing the growth of Pentecostalism, the actual development is far more complex. A survey of Pentecostalism shows it has developed a greater number of forms. Veli-Matti Kärkkäinen follows Vinson Synan's categorization by enumerating at least six theological streams.

First, "Wesleyan" Pentecostals emphasize "second blessing" instant sanctification, adding the baptism in the Holy Spirit evidenced by speaking in tongues as a "third blessing." Second, "Baptistic" Pentecostals came into being with the formation in America of the AG in 1914 emphasizing gradual sanctification, rather than an instant crisis experience. The AoG/ACC falls within this category. Third, "Oneness" Pentecostals teach a form of Unitarianism which denies the traditional doctrine of the Trinity. Most in this third group hold that tongues-speaking is necessary for salvation. Fourth, "Charismatics" who mostly stayed in their denominational church after the renewal of the Spirit, include aspects of Pentecostal practice and theology. Fifth, "Independent Charismatic" ministries that have diverse foci like the "Toronto Blessing," the "Pensacola Revival," and now the addition of the "Bethel" movement headed by Pastor Bill Johnson emphasizing the *experiential presence* of the Holy Spirit. Sixth, a variety of movements especially in the Majority World, add to the diversity; some are syncretistic and border on being non-Christian.[1]

It must also be understood that throughout its development, the Evangelical movement and its theology has also heavily influenced Pentecostalism in both its theology and spirituality. Due to the great diversity within the Pentecostal/Charismatic movement it is difficult to locate its defining unifying features or distinctive. Some definitions are too restrictive and link the term "Pentecostal" almost exclusively to the experience of the "baptism with the Holy Spirit." This is seen as the primary defining feature and reflects the doctrinal position of most classical Pentecostals. They usually believe in two distinct doctrines of "consequence" or "initial evidence" (that speaking in tongues is the consequence of or primary evidence of Spirit baptism), and "subsequence" (that Spirit baptism is a definite and subsequent experience to conversion). Some Charismatics have followed this teaching and are referred to as neo-Pentecostals, as their theology is similar to classical Pentecostals. From a global perspective it can be argued that this definition is too narrow and that a better approach is to look beyond Pentecostal/Charismatic theology's formulation, to empirical observations to clarify the distinctive features of Pentecostal spirituality. In this chapter various views and observations about Pentecostal spiritualities made by scholars, ministers and observers of the movement are surveyed and their key findings categorized into a number of main themes. It is acknowledged that most of the literature on this subject is from North America and Europe, although increasingly scholars are becoming aware of Pentecostalism's indigenous expressions worldwide.

Observations on Pentecostal Spirituality

The interaction between belief and behavior within the context of Scripture and contemporary culture helps us understand the specific nature of Pentecostal spirituality. Until recently, Pentecostals did not talk about their "spirituality"—it was not part of their vocabulary. Consequently, we have a concept of spirituality, which has a long background in the historic or mainline churches about the believer's growth in the life of the Holy Spirit and a shorter history of the various contemporary terms and expressions used in the Pentecostal movement such as "Spirit-filled," "baptism in the Spirit," "sanctified," "godly," and so forth.

1. Synan, "Origins of the Pentecostal Movement," 89–90.

Although the beginnings of Pentecostalism may be arbitrarily limited to a specific time frame, and a particular subculture and participants, it is in fact an expression of an ongoing tradition within Christianity[2] but in this past century it has become a major stream in Christianity. Amos Yong argues the explosion of the Pentecostal/Charismatic movement attests to the vitality of its pneumatocentric spirituality.[3] During the twentieth century it became the largest category in Protestantism. Catholics were the largest group at 50% of the worldwide church. Classical Pentecostals were the second largest at 20%.[4]

According to a Pew Forum analysis there are now about 279 million Pentecostal Christians and 305 million Charismatic Christians in the world. This means that, according to this analysis, Pentecostal and Charismatic Christians together make up about 27% of all Christians and more than 8% of the world's total population. The Pew Forum from the Center commissioned the figures in this report, dated December 2011 for the Study of Global Christianity at Gordon-Conwell Theological Seminary. The researchers generated estimates based in large part on figures provided by Christian organizations around the world.[5] Present trends indicate this is likely to rise to 1,140 million or 44% of the total number of Christians by 2025.[6] It is one of the most extraordinary religious phenomena in history. It is not surprising therefore that there are different perspectives on what constitutes the distinctive features of its spirituality! L. Grant McClung reveals that the Pentecostal/Charismatic movement comes in an astonishing variety of 38 major categories, 11,000 Pentecostal denominations, 3,000 independent Charismatic denominations in over 8,000 ethnolinguistic cultures and 7,000 languages.[7]

However, a number of distinct and essential features and motifs can be seen in different populations, cultures and environments. The central Pentecostal concern seems to be an emphasis on the "lived reality" of the Christian life through the experience of the indwelling power of the Spirit in the believer. At the heart of this spirituality is prayer, whereby people respond to God's revelation.

2. Wilson, "They Crossed the Red Sea," 107–8.
3. Yong, *Discerning the Spirit(s)*, 319.
4. Kärkkäinen, *Pneumatology*, 89.
5. Pew Forum, "Global Christianity," 67–69.
6. Barrett and Johnson, "Status of Global Mission," 2.
7. McClung, "Pentecostal/Charismatic Perspectives," 11.

The Distinctiveness of Pentecostal Spirituality

Primal Spirituality

Harvey Cox, one of the foremost observers of religions, sees Pentecostalism as a primal spirituality with three dimensions: *primal speech*, in glossolalia, a language of the heart; *primal piety*, in the resurgence of trance, vision, healing, dreams, dance, and other religious expressions; and *primal hope*, in Pentecostalism's millennial outlook which holds that a radical new age is about to dawn.[8] By "primal spirituality" Cox is referring to

> the core of human religiousness . . . that largely unprocessed nucleus of the psyche in which the unending struggle for a sense of purpose and significance goes on. Classical theologians have called it the "imago dei," the image of God in every person.[9]

Although at times Cox seems to interpret the Pentecostal experience as something purely latent in humans, Pentecostal spirituality actually involves a particular encounter with God's Spirit, not just any spirit. It is a primal spirituality but one uniquely based on a saving experience of Jesus Christ.[10] Cox claims the rise of Pentecostal spirituality is so significant in the reshaping of religion in the twenty-first century, he reversed his thesis position on increasing secularization, calling it an "unanticipated manifestation of the reappearance of primal spirituality in our time."[11]

African American Sources and Features

Scholars Steven Land, Walter Hollenweger, Veli-Matti Kärkkäinen and Allan Anderson, all identify the African American sources as the most important spiritualities affecting Pentecostalism's pioneers, giving rise to the movement of "participation in the Spirit."[12] Hollenweger explicates the five main features of this African American spirituality as: an oral liturgy; a narrative theology and witness; maximum participation of members in worship, service and decision making; dreams and visions in public worship; and the relationship between body and mind manifested by healing through prayer and liturgical dance. Anderson cites examples of African

---

8. Cox, *Fire from Heaven*, 81–122.
9. Ibid., 81.
10. Williams, "Harvey Cox and Pentecostalism," 25–26.
11. Cox, *Fire from Heaven*, 83.
12. Land, *Pentecostal Spirituality*; Hollenweger, "Black Roots"; Kärkkäinen, *Pneumatology*; Anderson, *Introduction to Pentecostalism*.

American Christian liturgy to include rhythmic hand clapping, the antiphonal participation of the congregation in the sermon, the sense of the immediacy of God in the services and baptism by immersion. All of these practices were fundamental to early Pentecostalism and remain common to varying degrees in Pentecostal churches worldwide to this day.[13] Both Anderson and Hollenweger believe the movement's growth in the Majority World is not because of adherence to a particular Pentecostal doctrine, but because of its roots in the spirituality of the nineteenth-century African American slave religion.[14] Only a quarter of Pentecostals are white and this is decreasing.[15]

Although Chant dismisses the oral/black tradition having any direct influence on the indigenous Australian Pentecostal movement,[16] it is argued that it would have impacted those overseas and American Pentecostals who traveled to Australia and subsequently influenced local Pentecostals. African American sources and features would have, at least on the view of the globalization of religion, influenced the Pentecostal movement in Australia, even if indirectly.

Experience of God in Liturgies and Rituals

Hollenweger asserts the strength of Pentecostalism is not in what Pentecostals conceptualize but in what the participants *experience* in their liturgies.[17] Pentecostal spirituality reflects the conviction that Pentecostals experience God through the Spirit and are expressed in liturgies that are mainly "oral, narrative and participatory."[18] Yong agrees that the experiential dimension of spirituality is expressed in these "oral, narrative and participatory" liturgies over and against an emphasis on "textuality." It is a pneumatocentric spirituality where the Spirit invades all life in various contexts, claiming to provide for more than the "spiritual" problems of life.[19]

Traditionally Pentecostals have rejected the words "liturgy" or "ritual" as they imply something "dead," meaningless, mechanical or religious, even

---

13. Anderson, *Introduction to Pentecostalism*, 43–44.
14. Anderson, "World Pentecostalism at a Crossroads," 20–33, 168.
15 Land, *Pentecostal Spirituality*, 21–22.
16. Chant, *Spirit of Pentecost*, 103.
17. Hollenweger, "Pentecostals and the Charismatic Movement," 549–54.
18. Anderson, *Introduction to Pentecostalism*, 201–2.
19. Yong, *Discerning the Spirit(s)*, 162, 319.

The Distinctiveness of Pentecostal Spirituality

unscriptural or un-spiritual. Ritual is spoken of as being too restrictive, routine and potentially inhibiting the Spirit's moving. However, Pentecostals do engage in rituals, though they often call them by other names such as: "praise and worship services," "Pentecostal distinctives," "tarry meetings," "altar calls," "laying on of hands" and so forth. "Ritual" has many definitions, but for the purpose of this study it represents those actions that a movement creates and sanctions as ways of behaving that express appropriate attitudes, values and beliefs within a given situation. In particular, *ritual* is applied to the *corporate worship service*. For contemporary Pentecostals, the church service lies at the heart of Pentecostal/Charismatic spirituality and constitutes its most central ritual.[20]

Daniel Albrecht researched Pentecostal/Charismatic "ritual" in three different types of local church: classical Pentecostal, neo-Pentecostal and Third Wave. Based on this study of "ritual" informed by ethnographic field research, he gives a descriptive interpretation of Pentecostal spirituality. Albrecht selected six fundamental emic or indigenous symbols, familiar idiomatic concepts rooted in Pentecostal parlance and ritual important to understanding Pentecostal spirituality; "leadership," "worship," "word," "gifts," "ministry" and "mission."[21]

Although Albrecht's descriptions are of churches in North America and might not be appropriate for all parts of the world, in my view it is applicable for those in the Western world. His methodology is pertinent because Pentecostal spirituality is best expressed in the actions of people at worship, prayer and ceremony. Much of his research confirms what other scholars had earlier claimed, but his findings are based in empirical studies. He distilled Pentecostal spirituality into eight areas.

First, it is a mystical/experiential piety, emphasizing encounter with the supernatural immanent sense of God's presence. Second, it accentuates an understanding that the "gifts of the Spirit," including the experience of "Spirit baptism," as normative church life. Third, it requires the category of

---

20. Albrecht, *Rites in the Spirit*, 21–24. He has an extensive list of Pentecostal rituals in his appendix A. Appendix B also lists and categorizes liturgical rites, foundational rites and micro-rites.

21. Albrecht, "Pentecostal Spirituality," 1–12. Anthropologists distinguish between emic and etic descriptions of culture. An emic term is one used by the people of a particular culture. An analysis utilizes folk terms and portrays the culture and its meanings from an insider's perspective. An etic analysis applies categories used to describe the culture to outsiders.

experience to understand it, particularly in worship.²² Church services are designed to provide a context for *encounter* with God's manifest presence. For Pentecostals, "worship" is another way of saying "presence of God."²³ God is experienced as the empowering Spirit who commissions through calling and gifting to service, mission and evangelism.²⁴ Fourth, it has a vitality of ritual that is less about structure than the embodied attitudes, the orientation, with which members engage in the rites as structured.²⁵ Fifth, it emphasizes celebration—God is experienced as creative, who encourages creativity marked by inventive and improvisational actions and an adaptable entrepreneurial spirit. Sixth, it has a strong element of "pragmatism" oriented to demonstrations of power for ministry. Seventh, it embodies an attitude of "contemplation" with a "deep receptivity" and encourages vulnerability and openness before God. Finally, it is rooted in a communal experience of God typified by the encouragement of democratic-participatory forms, seen in biblical symbols, orality and kinaesthetic/musical activity.²⁶

Albrecht finds the core of Pentecostal and Charismatic spirituality is a basic common belief in the immanent activity of God's Spirit and the essential goal of the Pentecostal church service is experiencing or encountering God. He concedes that no single treatment can encompass all the varieties of Pentecostal spiritualities.²⁷ Anderson agrees and adds that they are "centred on the experience of the Spirit that pervades the whole person."²⁸

These findings appear consistent with Chant's description of the distinctive features, pointing out that early Pentecostalism was insistent in nature, making it difficult to be a nominal member. There was an expectation to lift your hands in worship and join in singing in the Spirit. People experience God through the gifts of the Spirit, expecting he will speak to them, injecting a note of excitement and anticipation into the meeting.²⁹

22. Albrecht, *Rites in the Spirit*, 24, 29.

23. Ibid., 194–95.

24. Albrecht, "Pentecostal Spirituality," 12–19.

25. The term "rite" is used to refer to a portion or practice or actions of the service (e.g., the song service, receiving an offering, receiving water or Spirit baptism, laying on of hands, altar responses and so forth) recognized as a legitimate part of the overall ritual.

26. Albrecht, *Rites in the Spirit*, 194–95.

27. Ibid., 24–29. Albrecht's study was confined to three churches in North America but it is helpful as being closer to the cultural context of Australia than many in other non-Western environments.

28. Anderson, *Introduction to Pentecostalism*, 204.

29. Chant, *Heart of Fire*, 242–49; Chant, *Spirit of Pentecost*, 544.

The Distinctiveness of Pentecostal Spirituality

Experiencing the Fullness of the Spirit

Walter Hollenweger was one of the first to call for a more inclusive definition of Pentecostal spirituality than the doctrine of the "initial evidence."[30] He argued Pentecostalism is distinctively concerned with the experience of the working of the Holy Spirit and the practice of the spiritual gifts. Hollenweger and his researchers reaffirmed the primary place of the African American church at Azusa Street as the heart or "cradle" of Pentecostalism in the 1970s. Scholars are now increasingly starting to point out the early histories of Pentecostalism suffered from a "white racial bias" that ignored the influence of black culture and a "gender bias" overlooking women.[31]

He looks back to the early Pentecostals who overcame dogmatic differences by developing an ecumenical bond whose basis was experiencing the presence of the living God, the reality of the Holy Spirit. They did not try and work out theological problems because the only legitimate aim before the second coming of Jesus was to sanctify and unite the people of God and evangelize the world in a single generation. In Majority World Pentecostalism these elements are usually more important than dogma.[32]

For most Pentecostals and Charismatics today, this experience of the immanence of God in the fullness of the Spirit through prayer, worship and the gifts of the Spirit enabling believers to evangelize, is still a main characteristic.

Supernatural Experience of the Holy Spirit

In Veli-Matti Kärkkäinen's view Pentecostalism is a new grassroots spiritual movement rather than one producing new theological constructions. "It has not so much produced a new theology as a new kind of spirituality and aggressive new evangelism methods."[33] His view of this spirituality can be condensed into four aspects. First, it involves the present-day normative manifestation of Spiritual gifts including miraculous healing, glossolalia and prophecy as bestowed by the Holy Spirit. It is the "revalorization of the charismata" rather than theological analysis that is its most important contribution. Second, a dynamic enthusiasm is reintroduced to the

---

30. Hollenweger, *Pentecostals*, 149.
31. Anderson, *Introduction to Pentecostalism*, 168–83.
32. Ibid., 19–20.
33. Kärkkäinen, *Introduction to Ecclesiology*, 70.

church focusing on experiencing God as supernatural. Third, empowerment through the Spirit for witnessing and service is emphasized, a factor in the movement's growth. Finally, Pentecostal worship emphasizes the supernatural.[34] AoG minister David Cartledge made the observation that Pentecostals expect the God who supernaturally reveals himself at conversion will continue to do so. "Speaking in tongues, immediately creates in the new Pentecostal an expectation of further supernatural and personal revelation."[35]

Implicit Values

Russell Spittler enumerates five implicit key values that govern Pentecostal spirituality quite apart from the common central features of speaking in tongues, the baptism in the Holy Spirit, and prayer for divine healing. Spittler gives an extensive list of Pentecostal practices, such as oral prayer, fasting, raising of hands, proxy prayer, laying on of hands, dancing in the Spirit, the Jericho march, altar services, falling under the power, sacred expletives, word of knowledge, anointed prayer cloths, holy laughter, exorcisms, dreams and visions and other fringe practices.[36]

First, the most constant value is individual "experience" including emotions of sorrow or joy. Second, "orality" is a basic quality of Pentecostal piety. Third, "spontaneity" is greatly valued as it is the Holy Spirit who moves unpredictably, guides worship and leads each believer (John 3:9). Fourth, "otherworldliness" is a strong feature but appears to be fading among Western Pentecostals. It has been argued the deprivation of early Pentecostals in the United States controlled their cosmology; the real world is the eternal one and it informed their eschatology that Christ would return any moment to put right wrongs. It may explain their little formed social conscience (1 John 2:17). Social justice was part of the church's eschatological hope rather than mission.[37]

Finally, a fifth value is a strong commitment to "biblical authority" that is more about the authoritative role of Scripture than complex arguments about the inerrant quality of the biblical text. The high regard for biblical authority and a tendency to take Scripture's words at face value explains

34. Kärkkäinen, *Pneumatology*, 90–92.
35. Cartledge, *Apostolic Revolution*, 17.
36. Spittler, "Spirituality, Pentecostal and Charismatic," 1099–102.
37. Ibid., 1101–2.

The Distinctiveness of Pentecostal Spirituality

many beliefs and practices.[38] Western Pentecostal academics emphasize "correct" biblical hermeneutics and written theology but most Pentecostals rely on an experiential understanding of the Bible.[39]

These five values were evident in the research of early AoG/ACC (Pentecostal) spirituality. In the next chapter our examination of contemporary Pentecostal spirituality will look at whether these values still have the same prominence.

Passion for the Kingdom

While acknowledging the contributions of Hollenweger and Spittler, Steven Land shows the relationship between spirituality and Pentecostal theology and defines the essential spirituality of Pentecostalism as "the integration of beliefs and practices in the affections which are themselves evoked and expressed by those beliefs and practices."[40] Land sees the "already–not yet" tension as important in understanding the power of this Pentecostal spirituality that is apocalyptic, corporate, missional and essentially affective. The center point of the spirituality is to experience life as part of the biblical drama of participation in God's history. This "passion for the kingdom" is the way Land describes Pentecostal spirituality centered in the experience of the "lived reality by the eschatological, missionary community, expressed by prayer and integrated by 'apocalyptic affections.'"[41] Whether contemporary Pentecostal pastors can be described as having such a passion for the kingdom as part of their Pentecostal spirituality will be explored in the next chapter.

Glossolalia (Tongues-Speaking)

From its inception, the distinctive feature of Pentecostalism has been the baptism in the Holy Spirit with the accompanying sign of *glossolalia* (Greek *glossa* = "tongue," *laleo* = "I speak"). For early or classical Pentecostals it is part of the process of Christian initiation; first, repentance and faith in Christ; second, baptism in water by immersion; third, baptism or infilling

---

38. Ibid., 1097–102.
39. Anderson, *Introduction to Pentecostalism*, 225–28.
40. Land, *Pentecostal Spirituality*, 38–39.
41. Ibid., 13–14, 56, 74–75, 218–19.

of the Holy Spirit, the initial sign of which is speaking in tongues. It means the ability to pray in a language that has never been learned and it is normally ongoing. It is seen as a gift of the Spirit, a nonrational expression of worship in words from the human spirit rather than the mind (1 Cor 14:14f.). The phenomenon may be accompanied by emotional expressions such as tears or laughter or trembling. On the basis of 1 Corinthians 13:1, Pentecostals have argued that the languages they speak may be either human or heavenly in nature.[42]

Sociologist Margaret Poloma defines glossolalia as a paranormal experience that is viewed as normative within Pentecostalism. After summarizing the various views of sociological researchers she presents her findings that support the contention that glossolalia is a religious experience that "breaks through social structures and functions to legitimize participation in religious institutions."[43] Although little sociological or psychological research has been done in Australia on glossolalia, Chant argues that the contemporary research can be applied to the Australian scene to understand its origins. He examines various theological and sociological perspectives on glossolalia, including its sacramental significance for Pentecostals. He questions whether the biblical writers would see glossolalia as an innate human ability; it was only "as the Spirit enabled them" that the disciples spoke in tongues (Acts 2:4). Examples cited by Chant clearly show the early Pentecostals had no doubt that glossolalia was a supernatural gift from God. He further examines early beliefs in *xenolalia* and concludes there is little evidence that Australian Pentecostals believed they could preach in tongues, but the conviction that tongues-speaking could be understood if you understood the language was prevalent. After examining a number of theories for understanding the phenomena, he points out that the biblical word *glossa* means "tongue" or "language" not mouthing nonsense syllables. That tongue-speech may be an altered state of consciousness, does not invalidate glossolalia any more than it invalidates prayer. In response to arguments that tongue-speakers are mentally or emotionally deficient, Chant points to investigations that have shown a high degree of emotional and psychological stability among glossolalics. He refers to the richness of language and vocabulary often employed in tongues speech as stretching the credulity of explanations about tongues-speaking having sub-conscious origins (like a child copying language sounds). He appears to agree with

---

42. Chant, *Spirit of Pentecost*, 83–85.
43. Poloma, *Assemblies of God*, 27, 36–39.

The Distinctiveness of Pentecostal Spirituality

Cox's view that tongues-speaking is a form of primal spirituality or pre-conceptual prayer—it is satisfying but not intellectually meaningful. Chant refers to examples of crying, joy and laughter common in early Pentecostal meetings and cited in *Good News* that support tongues-speaking as the language of feeling; "groans that words cannot express" (Rom 8:26). He concludes that the various theories add weight to the view that glossolalia is a natural human experience reactivated by the Spirit. He acknowledges the theories do not explain how it works or where the ability to speak fluently in a language never learned originates from.[44]

Chant notes that the rising incidence of glossolalia has paralleled the rise of rationalism, indicating what Pentecostals have been saying all along, that religion is not essentially a matter of the mind but the heart. He concludes the practice of glossolalia is recognition of the place and validity of experience in religion. His thesis attempts to show that Pentecostalism not only encourages people to experience the presence of God but to enshrine that experience in an audible, visible, sacramental and sanctifying encounter called the baptism in the Holy Spirit.[45] Glossolalia counters a purely cognitive or rationalistic approach to spirituality yet it satisfies the need for observable criteria. It can be measured, being experienced by the speaker and observed by others; it has both subjective and objective aspects. The results of the survey of AoG Pentecostal pastors considered in the next chapter provide measures of frequencies of glossolalia among pastors, enabling an inference to be drawn of the direction that the practice is heading.

Postscript on Postmodernism

Partly through the influence of postmodern thought, there is a greater recognition of the importance of *experience* in defining reality. Theology is now beginning to recognize that experience is an authentic source of divine revelation. When scholars "describe a singular 'Pentecostal spirituality' as the experience of God through the Spirit, this transcends cultural boundaries and provides an authentic, yet flexible encounter with God that is meaningful in its different cultural expressions."[46] Johns argues Pentecostalism has actually anticipated the postmodern revolution, by opening the

---

44. Chant, *Spirit of Pentecost*, 85–96.
45. Ibid., 83–98.
46. Sheldrake, *Spirituality and History*, 41; Anderson, *Introduction to Pentecostalism*, 195–96, 200, 204.

realms of reality, which exist outside objective, scientific knowledge.[47] For the purposes of this discussion, postmodernism may be understood as a reaction to, and development from modernism. Os Guinness, an Evangelical, describes the phenomenon as a break with modernism:

> Where modernism was a manifesto of human self-confidence and self-congratulation, postmodernism is a confession of modesty if not despair. There is no truth, only truths. There are no principles, only preferences. There is no grand reason, only reasons.[48]

Postmodernism can be described as the expansion of reason to include the nonrational and spiritual dimensions of human personality.[49] One of the attractive aspects of it for the Pentecostal is that it appears to make space for an encounter with God which modernism would not do.[50] Robinson claims Pentecostals have much to offer a Western world that is "throwing off a secular worldview in favour of a religious encounter that is essentially neo-pagan."[51]

Wonsuk Ma argues Postmodernism is appealing to some Pentecostals because it provides legitimacy for an intuitive reading of Scripture. The immediacy of God's word in Scripture has long been a Pentecostal value, even before the term "postmodernism" became popular. Ma says the great interest in spirituality that paradoxically exists in a postmodern world opens up many opportunities to Pentecostals to address such issues as institutionalization, social concerns, inclusion of women in ministry, global mission, racial reconciliation, and the renewal of the early Pentecostals' vision of a healthy ecumenical relationship with other Christians.[52]

Cargal argues all that is needed for Pentecostals to enter into the postmodern age is to throw off their Fundamentalist and Evangelical shackles.[53] Menzies's considered response is that although postmodernism has much to offer, its ahistorical stance and epistemological skepticism is extreme and leads to relativism.[54] The challenge for Pentecostals is to nurture their

---

47. Johns, *Pentecostalism and the Postmodern Worldview*, 87.
48. Guinness, *Fit Bodies Fat Minds*, 103.
49. Bosch, *Transforming Mission*, 350–62.
50. Clark, "Pentecostal Hermeneutics," 88.
51. Robinson, "Response to Critical Issues," 195.
52. Ma, "Biblical Studies," 63–64.
53. Cargal, "Beyond the Fundamentalist-Modernist Controversy," 163–87.
54. Menzies, *Spirit and Power*, 63–64.

experiential heritage without falling into open-ended subjectivity. As Guinness warns, postmodernism is based on a philosophical position, which challenges Pentecostal theologizing. Although it appears more sympathetic to religion than modernism on the surface, "it is naive to ignore the price tag." Postmodernism allows all religions and beliefs to present and practice their claims but "demands the relinquishing of any claims to unique, absolute, and transcendent truth."[55] For many Christians, including Pentecostals, the price tag would be too great.

Classical and Current Pentecostal Spirituality

My survey of the literature has found considerable consistency as to the essential features of Pentecostal (including AoG/ACC) spirituality. The importance of *experience* of the Spirit in Pentecostal spirituality is paramount and this has always been the case in Australia. It is not just about forms and formal procedures but also about living a Christian way of life. Although the "lived spirituality" of Pentecostals is broader, classical Pentecostals usually have defined themselves in narrower terms by the doctrine of speaking in tongues as the "initial evidence" of the baptism in the Holy Spirit. This classical view is the formal and written doctrinal position of Pentecostal denominations. Spirit baptism is seen as a distinct experience subsequent to conversion and followed by tongues-speaking as the initial evidence.

Despite its emphasis on experience Pentecostalism was from its beginnings, and still is today, influenced by Evangelicalism and its literary expressions of doctrine, theology and faith. There is, however, a continuing tension when developments in Pentecostalism seek to enshrine its spirituality (beliefs and practices), into such "codified" written forms. Many see this as evidence of institutionalization. This began very early on in the new movement. The question of whether this is a continuing and an adverse influence on faith and ministry will be considered later.

In the next chapter, we will seek to discover if the classical position has changed in recent actual practice and beliefs of pastors today. In my doctoral research, the spirituality (practices and beliefs) of one current Western Pentecostal denomination, the AoG/ACC, was measured and examined. The aim was to discover whether the current practice of its pastors indicated they were confining themselves to the classical written doctrinal position, or whether their emphasis was more on the *experience* of the

---

55. Guinness, *Fit Bodies Fat Minds*, 106–7.

working of the Holy Spirit and the *exercise* of spiritual gifts. Change from the classical position may indicate a reaction by AoG/ACC pastors against the early institutionalization of doctrine, or it may simply be a sign that more mainline expressions are being adopted.

Specifically, the research considered whether or not there is more or less emphasis on the classical Pentecostal experiences, attitudes, beliefs and practices by pastors. Are more or less mainstream (non-Pentecostal) forms of private devotional practices being adopted? Has there been a drift toward "Charismatic" and "Third Wave," beliefs and approaches? Are pastors indicating an increase or decrease in Pentecostal practices in church services? What is occurring in relation to involvement in community services and outreach? Both qualitative and quantitative data was examined in an attempt to determine what are current pastors' practices and beliefs and how they relate to accepted early Pentecostal spirituality—its oral, narrative and participatory liturgies, supernatural experience of God, experience of the fullness of the Spirit, implicit values, affective passions integrated in Pentecostal beliefs and practice, glossolalia and, the "initial evidence" doctrine.

4

Contemporary Pentecostal Spirituality

Introduction

THE ESSENTIAL FEATURES OF Pentecostal spirituality were ascertained in the previous chapter. They evidenced a number of different aspects and manifestations that can be observed, described, measured and discussed. In this chapter, developments in more recent times, particularly with regard the practices and experiences in my own context of Australian Pentecostal pastors (AoG), will be examined to see if there has been any change in their Pentecostal spirituality. Summarized results of the national survey of senior pastors on their spiritual experiences and practices will be presented. Further information from anecdotal materials of key leaders in the AoG movement on their experiences of the Spirit in the past and present will be considered. Their reflections on the results of the survey and observations on current Pentecostal spirituality will be looked at. The views of scholars and commentators will also be considered. In the final chapters the effects of any institutionalization and the ramifications of any change in Pentecostal spirituality will be explored involving sociological, biblical and theological insights.

Recent Developments

As previously discussed, for early Pentecostals, spiritual experiences both at the corporate and individual levels were emphasized, the most important being glossolalia. Even today an AoG/ACC pastor's credential application still requires pastors to state whether they have experienced the baptism in the Holy Spirit and "speak with tongues as the Spirit gives utterance as the initial evidence" before being ordained.[1]

Despite this ongoing emphasis on the experience of the Holy Spirit, the early Pentecostal churches remained relatively few in numbers for many years. "Pentecostal churches prior to 1960 were as a matter of course, fairly small."[2] David Cartledge, an AoG National Executive member for twenty years, asserts one reason for this was "a rapid development of the denominationalism that the founders deplored," resulting in the erosion of the autonomy of local churches.[3] Although this claim is debatable, nevertheless it is possible that institutionalization may have adversely impacted the AoG and perhaps influenced its spiritual practices and beliefs. Cartledge claims there was a positive change in the renewal and growth of the AoG in the 1970s due to the "restoration of the Charismatic ministries of apostles and prophets," in contrast to these offices being formalized positions in a denominational system. His reasoning is that whereas the early Pentecostals accepted these dynamic ministries, the next generation of classical Pentecostal leaders reacted against prophetic ministry during the middle decades of the century in response to their abuse and misuse. He says that in North America by the 1940s, the Assemblies of God in the USA (AG) had shifted toward Evangelicalism, adopting an "ultra conservative posture"—a more restrained approach was taken that resulted in the marginalization of any experiences of personal prophecy. He argued this adversely influenced the Pentecostal movement around the world, including Australia. One study of the AG in America claims the decrease of those who claim to have received the baptism in the Holy Spirit with the "initial physical evidence" of speaking in tongues to a low 40% is due to the influence of the Charismatic renewal, theological challenges from Bruner (1970), Dunn (1970) and others, and the "evangelicalization" of the AG, but none of these assertions have been scientifically tested.[4]

Cartledge claims that certain developments in Australia ensured the AoG did not go the same way as North America. In the 1970s the AoG was

---

1. See Article 5:13 of the United Constitution in the *Assemblies of God in Australia 1993: Constitutional Documents (Including AOG World Missions Missionary Constitution)*, April 1993.
2. Hutchinson, "New Thing God Is Doing," 7.
3. Cartledge, *Apostolic Revolution*, 123.
4. Ibid., 35–38, 47–51.

experiencing tension over the influence of the Charismatic renewal with two streams emerging, both for and against, this "new move." A renewal of Pentecostal/Charismatic manifestations and practices such as "freer worship," "singing in the spirit," "dancing before the Lord," "prostration," "deliverance," "prophecy," "visions," and "holy laughter" began to occur in churches.[5] A fractious AoG National Conference in 1973 over these manifestations of the Spirit resulted in disagreement over the autonomy of the Australian churches. A proposal for a North American-styled centralized administrative system, involving full-time bureaucratic leaders, was rejected in favor of appointing Executive leaders who also actively led their own churches. Cartledge believes this preserved the autonomy of the AoG and released truly "apostolic and prophetic ministries" to develop their own networks of churches.[6] For instance, the former AoG/ACC president, Brian Houston, leads the largest national church, heads up his own international network of churches and hosts *Hillsong Conference* with more registrants than the AoG/ACC National Conference.

One report stated that the 1973 Executive unanimously agreed that the spiritual vitality of people, rather than administrative structure and constitutional change, is where emphasis should be placed to ensure renewal. Clearly, however, decisions were made for structural change to facilitate renewal. It was decided to reduce the Executive Presbytery to seven members and change the nature of the Executive to ensure that the secretary/treasurer became the only full-time position instead of the general superintendent.[7]

Shane Clifton's view is that during the 1970s and 1980s the AoG underwent its largest transition from congregational democratic ecclesiology to pastor-led churches. He believes this originated from the influence of the Charismatic movement and the rapid growth that accompanied this renewal when many in mainline churches began to experience the baptism in the Holy Spirit with speaking in tongues. Clifton refers to denominational articles in the 1970s supporting the view that the charismatic renewal was generally celebrated by the AoG as a work of the Spirit of God and was within the spirit of Pentecost.[8] Although the AoG had grown to only 120

---

5. Ibid., 125–26.
6. Ibid., 134, 149–51.
7. Smith and Smith, *River Is Flowing*, 60–63.
8. Clifton, "Apostolic Revolution." See also Garlock, "Spreading Flame of Pentecost," *Evangel* 27 (1970) 9–11, and Macpherson, "Pentecostal Signs," *Evangel* 29 (1972) 10–12.

churches by 1972, the next few years saw a second period of renewal with a surge to nearly two hundred churches by 1979.

Hutchinson believes the reason for growth in the Pentecostal churches at this time was due to significant transfer growth, particularly during 1976–1981, "as almost all mainline denominations hardened their attitudes towards charismatics."[9] Not all the Pentecostal church growth came from Charismatic transfer but it is reasonable to infer that a big jump in numbers in 1979–1981 was mainly due to this. During a six-year period that saw a "decay in charismatic forms and membership—between 1973 and 1979," the AoG grew by 3,552 members. In two years (1979–1981) it grew by over 13,000 members and has sustained this growth in absolute numbers. By 1993 there were 97,654 members, 717 churches and 1,404 ministers—growth goals to 110,000 were reached in 1995.[10]

In 1984, Chant also thought this growth in the seventies and eighties was in part influenced by the Charismatic movement and also by a new professional approach to church development.[11] This growth rate appears supported by AoG's statistics. During Andrew Evans' term as General Superintendent (1977–1997), the AoG grew to 700 churches from 152 churches and 9,446 constituents in 1977.[12] By 1984, there were 356 churches with 44,863 attenders.[13] Between 1973–1980 members grew from 7,302 to 20,715. In 1970 there were 110 congregations and by 1986 there were five times that number.[14]

Although Cartledge argued that a move away from democratic type structures encouraged the growth in the movement, it was more likely that the increase in the size and number of churches was facilitated from the Charismatic renewal and the church growth emphasis. It was this growth that "necessitated structural change, which in a circular fashion, then facilitated further church growth." Larger churches responded by vesting governmental authority in the senior pastor and church board/eldership. Smaller churches followed adopting similar structures in anticipation of

---

9. Hutchinson, "New Thing God Is Doing," 7–8.
10. Ibid., 12.
11. Chant, *Heart of Fire*, 144–45.
12. *AOG Website* 2004, 1.
13. *Ministers Bulletin*, 4.
14. Smith and Smith, *River Is Flowing*, 71, 83.

growth. As an executive member, Cartledge would have been involved in promoting these changes.[15]

Although the Pentecostal movement was still increasing numerically, by 1999 Chant was arguing that a significant Pentecostal growth *rate* of 87.9% (compared with a 7.5% population growth rate) for 1976–81 was slowing markedly. The next five years it was still a healthy 48% but by 1991–1996, it had dropped to 16%. This was the case even though overall numbers were still growing. Chant acknowledges there may be many reasons for this decline, but he questions whether there is a correlation with a softening of the need for tongues as sign of being baptized in the Spirit in that same period.[16] This seems to indicate there was a significant change occurring in Pentecostal spirituality. Hutchinson also saw the growth rate was slowing for the AoG. He believed this was partly due to the addition to ever larger numbers in the main body of the church. In his view the National Church Life Survey indicated an increase in nominal Pentecostalism suggesting that the forces of institutionalization at work.[17] My research was conducted with the hope that the data would clarify whether the pastors' Pentecostal spirituality was changing and whether this was because of the impact of institutionalization.

The newest category of renewal to impact the AoG is the "Third Wave" of the Spirit, which originated at Fuller Theological Seminary in 1981 under the ministry of John Wimber. By 1990, this "Third Wave" numbered thirty-three million members.[18] This consists of mainline Evangelicals who said "signs and wonders" (including tongues) were to be sought as evidence of the Spirit's indwelling at conversion. However, they do not consider themselves as Pentecostal or Charismatic being opposed to a dogmatic position on "consequence" and "subsequence." They acknowledge the gifts of the Spirit, including tongues, without the need for a baptism in the Spirit after conversion as it is assumed all the gifts are received at conversion and remain latent until subsequently released by teaching and service. This objection may be due to suspicion of the Wesleyan roots of Pentecostalism with fear of a reemergence of the teaching of entire sanctification, which caused much damage in the early twentieth century.[19]

15. Clifton, "Holy Spirit," 7.
16. Chant, *Spirit of Pentecost*, 545.
17. Hutchinson, "New Thing," 12.
18. Synan, "Origins of the Pentecostal Movement," 12.
19. See Piggin, *Evangelical Christianity in Australia*, 105–25.

Ian Jagelman warned "Third Wavers" actually pose the greatest internal challenge if allowed to penetrate Pentecostal church leadership structures. He argued that they will subtly undermine the need for the baptism in the Holy Spirit with the result that spiritual gifts will gradually disappear from Pentecostal spirituality.[20]

Another controversial "renewal" influence emerged in the mid-1990s called the "Toronto Blessing." It came from Toronto Airport Vineyard Church in Canada, led by John Arnott. It has impacted many churches worldwide,[21] including Australia. Arnott had visited Claudio Freidzon of the AG in Argentina, where there had been a revival with unusual manifestations including "holy laughter" and "falling under the power." These became marks of Toronto, but they have been reported in many Pentecostal meetings over the past century. Whether this new movement will have the lasting effect of other great revivals in history is still to be seen.

Chant argues that in the pre-World War II years in Australian Pentecostalism, the baptism in the Holy Spirit was seen as a vital spiritual experience that rested firmly on biblical foundations. He argues that with the emergence of the "Charismatic," the "Third Wave" movements and the "Toronto Blessing," there has been a focus on the value of an *emotional experience* for its own sake, rather than as a sign of spiritual empowering. Chant believes a preoccupation with *experience* rather than a clear focus on glossolalia as sign of the impartation of the Holy Spirit is corrosive. However, he cites the fact that the official *Assemblies of God Statement of Faith* has not changed, as some indication that a significant element of the Pentecostal movement has retained its traditional stance.[22] However, it appears that the survey data and other data provided may challenge this view.

Hutchinson believes increasing diversity in the AoG was eating at its identity as a Pentecostal movement:

> Theologically, the Church traditions which the charismatic refugees of the late 1970s brought into the Pentecostal Churches also relativized the two great cornerstones of the Azusa Street tradition—tongues, which became not "the" but "a" marker of the baptism of the Holy Spirit, and restorationism.

---

20. Jagelman, "Church Growth," 36.
21. Anderson, *Introduction to Pentecostalism*, 164–65.
22. Chant, *Spirit of Pentecost*, 545–46.

The research detailed below seeks to uncover whether there is evidence to indicate any change in actual practice of the pastors' Pentecostal spirituality, if not in any official doctrinal statements.

Changes in Style and Structure

In recent years, the AoG/ACC appears to have moved toward more professional, structured and controlled patterns of leadership. At the same time however, there has generally been a fresh dynamic in worship services, openness to non Anglo-Celtic cultural groups, and an attempt to present a more relevant interface with the community. The national leadership has allowed some diversity and the development of various trends within the movement. Generally it has avoided divisiveness over potentially problematic issues, such as "dancing before the Lord," "singing in the spirit," "holy laugher," "contemporary music," and the invitation of guest ministries. This approach has been at a time of growth again. By April 2003, the AoG exceeded 1,000 churches. The AoG National Secretary claimed it as the largest increase of any two-year period.[23] Official statistics claim "1,012 churches with over 160,000 constituents."[24] The National Conference in May 2005 announced a total of 1,076 churches.[25] The 2001 NCLS Occasional Paper no. 3, by J. Bellamy and K. Castle, February 2004, estimates weekly attendance for the AoG to be 104,600 in 2001, 6.9% of weekly church attendance in Australia, a 20% increase since 1996.

As at December 2015 the Assemblies of God in Australia website states that the denomination which "was formed in 1937 has experienced consistent growth. It adopted a new name of *Australian Christian Churches* in 2007 and currently consists of over 1,000 churches with over 280,000 constituents, making it the largest Pentecostal movement in Australia."[26] The latest annual overview from National President Wayne Alcorn, dated 19 November 2015, reveals that there are "well over 310,000 constituents in ACC churches" (over 8% growth), 32% (almost a third) of ACC churches have been planted since 2006, and 50% of all ACC churches were founded since 2000.[27]

---

23. Ainge, "AOG Exceeds 1,000," 8–9.
24. AOG website, "About Us," http://www.acc.org.au/about-us.
25. Cettolin, unpublished notes.
26. AOG website, "About Us," http://www.acc.org.au/about-us.
27. Alcorn, "ACC Overview."

Non-Executive, so-called "apostolic and prophetic" ministries have proliferated running music concerts, conferences and outreaches such as "Youth Alive" and "Planet Shakers." Christine Westwood's interpretation of this phenomena, in the *Australian*, is that "religious music is going back to its traditional role of capturing the heart and moving the soul" as Wesley did in the eighteenth century, making Christian music accessible by adapting popular tunes.[28] From the mid-1980s a new stream of music came out of Hillsong Church, Sydney, that has had a large influence on many churches worldwide. The *News Briefs* section of the AOG's *Now!* magazine reports over 18,000 delegates from 70 nations at Hillsong's 2005 Conference. Most denominations in Australia were represented and 2,700 volunteers involved. Sessions covered the arts, music, leadership and community work.[29] It is Australia's largest megachurch[30] founded in in 1983 with forty-five members, and now claims over 25,000 members with churches and offices in major cities in five continents. The Hillsong's annual Sydney conference draws in excess of 28,000 people, the European counterpart in London about 16,000.[31]

The pressure of growth and to grow resulted in many AoG churches changing their governmental style from "congregational," with power vested in a board of elders over the senior minister, to a "leadership driven" model where the pastor works with a board driven by a vision statement and values. Cartledge argued change from congregational government to leadership by those with ministry gifts and ministry teams is one of the most significant developments in the AoG.[32] Churches have a variety of ministry gifts and functions leading to diversity in church life and emphasis.[33] A recent increase in females taking on pastoral roles has also occurred but nowhere near as many proportionally as in the earliest days of the Pentecostal movement in Australia. Over twice the number of women hold ministry credentials today than in 1977. Most work in ministry teams or with spouses but some are, senior pastors or solo ministers.[34]

28. Westwood, "Psalm Remains the Same," 14.
29. *Now!*, 14.
30. A megachurch is generally defined as a church with over 2,000 members.
31. Riches and Wagner, "Evolution of Hillsong Music," n.p.
32. Cartledge, *Apostolic Revolution*, 403.
33. Ibid., 381–408.
34. Until Melinda Dwight's election in 1998, there had never been a woman on the Victoria/Tasmanian State Executive. National Executive member and Hillsong pastor

Business Review Weekly described Pentecostal churches, as a "new breed of Christianity sweeping Australia and spawning churches that are among the country's fastest-growing and most entrepreneurial."[35] A third period of growth in the AoG has been identified from the time of Brian Houston's election in May 1997 as National President. The average church size increased to 147, with church planting also continuing.

Clifton argues that during the course of the twentieth century the AoG/ACC has moved away from loose-knit voluntarist communities to congregationalist free-church structures, and to recently adopting ecclesiologies labelled as "Apostolic Revolution or Reformation" that focus both local church and inter-church authority in the hands of influential church leaders. These changes have been motivated in the main by the mission of proclaiming the gospel to a rapidly developing Australian society. Although they may have enabled the AoG/ACC to harness the substantial growth in Pentecostalism during the last century, they may have also resulted in a move away from the ideals and values significant to previous generations of Pentecostals.[36]

New Networks

The AoG became the major founding member of *Australian Christian Churches* which began as a new "loose umbrella organization" of several co-operating Pentecostal denominations committed to communicating Christianity within Australian society through relevant ways and practical community care. After his election as president, Brian Houston was instrumental in launching this network aiming to change the public's perception of churches, facilitate inter-church relationships and share resources. Currently 430 church-based agencies provide over 2000 welfare services. It claimed the second highest attendances after Catholics, with over 200,000 people attending 1200 affiliated churches weekly.[37]

However, the *Australian Christian Churches* network's stated aim was to move away from representing Pentecostalism *per se* and to embrace all

---

Donna Crouch is as at 2015 the only female on a State or National Executive. See also Jim Reiher's article, "Women's Participation in Victorian Church Leadership," *Australasian Pentecostal Studies* 7 (2003) 5.

35. Ferguson, "Prophet-Minded," 35.
36. Clifton, "Apostolic Revolution and the Ecclesiology of the AoGA," n.p.
37. *AOG Website* 2004, 1–6.

churches that seek to reach their communities in a culturally relevant way. It recognized diversity in the common mission and key points of theology that "all Christian Churches share." It claimed to be classically biblical in doctrine; to be charismatic in expression; to embrace the gifts of the Spirit but focused to reach others; to be contemporary in style and relevance; to be "pro-active in care" with churches not just for members but for the community.[38] It was announced at the latest AoG National Conference in Sydney on 4 May 2005 that this network intended to broaden its appeal to all like-minded Australian contemporary churches and not be limited to Charismatic and Pentecostal churches. However, it required forming another organization as the AoG wished to retain ownership of the ACC name.[39] The new goal was to bring together all contemporary churches representing about 400,000 people.[40] However the network was not appealing to all Pentecostal movements, perhaps fearing a loss of autonomy or independence and the initiative lost momentum. The AoG subsequently abandoned the pursuit of the loose umbrella organization of like-minded contemporary Christian churches and changed its own denominational name in 2007 from *Assemblies of God in Australia* to *Australian Christian Churches* (ACC).

Social and Political Involvement

Before the turn of the last century, the AoG rarely took steps to get involved in social justice issues or political involvement but in recent years it invited political leaders to take them more seriously. A number of AoG members and other Pentecostal members have also stood for political office, some successfully. Prime Minister John Howard opened Hillsong Church's building in October 2002. Federal Treasurer Peter Costello accepted an invitation to address the Hillsong Conferences in 2004 and 2005 before 28,000 registrants. Former AoG National Superintendent Andrew Evans was elected into the South Australian Parliament and Steve Fielding, a member of City Life, an independent ACC church, was elected to the Federal Senate representing Victoria. Both were elected as members of the Family First Party. Articles in the November 2001 edition of *Australian Christian Churches News* magazine evidence development into areas of advocacy for the poor and social

38. Ibid.
39. Cettolin, unpublished notes.
40. Ferguson, "Prophet-Minded," 37.

welfare. Articles report: the Prime Minister welcoming the *National Day of Honour* initiative; social justice "in the power of the Holy Spirit;" chaplaincy work; community awards to church-based volunteers; "the Christian and politics"; Australian Christian Care Network; Hillsong's forty community welfare ministries and; Pentecostals redefining faith-based work.[41]

Worship Music

Riches and Wagner have studied the development of Hillsong Music over the life of the church from its inception identifying four phases of brand development: Phase 1, Geoff Bullock's Songs and Leadership (1985–1995); Phase 2, Darlene Zschech and Hillsong's International Fame (1995–1997); Phase 3, the Emergence of United (1998–2002); Phase 4, Hillsong London and International Bands (2003–2007); Phase 5, Consolidation of the Hillsong Brand (2008–2012). In these researchers' estimation,

> while the total number of songs increased over years references to conversion were greater than the general increase, however Spirit Baptism decreased in phases two, three, and four.... Hillsong emphasized evangelical doctrine in its music during phase four, with ecumenical intent HMA songs rarely address the Spirit directly, despite the total increase of songs across the phases. The reduction of songs addressing the Spirit is also evidence of the consideration of . . . reaching an increasingly broad audience . . . lyrical references moving away from individual supernatural empowerment towards the church as Spirit empowered to effect social transformation within the community.... As churches grow they are often forced to accommodate a broader range of views within their congregation. Also, increased ecumenical contact leads to a softening of views on issues deemed controversial.[42]

Today most AoG/ACC churches are heavily reliant on using Hillsong music and choruses in their worship services.

A Fundamental Change

It appears the influence of the Charismatic renewal and neo-Pentecostal movements and the impact of growth have significantly influenced a

---

41. *ACC News*, 2001.
42. Riches and Wagner, "Evolution of Hillsong Music."

classical Pentecostal denomination with mixed results. The recent changes in the AoG/ACC, are going beyond simply matters of style, leadership and church structure, but are symptomatic of a fundamental change in its Pentecostal spirituality.

Poloma's research on the AG in North America found it was the local church where prophetic gifts are nurtured and is vital in regulating the tension that exists between charisma and structure. She found that local church pastors in touch with the needs of their church power base are the key to curbing threats that over-institutionalization pose to charisma. Her findings would have application to a comparable Western context in Australia.[43] If so, then the local church pastor may be the key to the development trajectory of the AoG/ACC's Pentecostal spirituality. Data from the national survey of AoG pastors will provide further information to inform the contemporary picture of their spirituality.

Survey of Pastors

The national survey of AoG pastors on Pentecostal spirituality conducted in 2004 and included questions on the size of the pastors' churches. The responses correlate reasonably with the denomination's statistics, supporting my contention that the survey provided a representative sample of churches and pastors. Forty-four percent had less than one hundred people, while 63% are in churches of two hundred or less.[44] Seventy-eight percent of the pastors had completed some program of study in a Bible College. At the time of the survey the AoG highly recommended, but stopped short of mandating, that pastoral credential candidates complete a Bible college course. It now requires the equivalent of one year's full-time theological studies as a condition for the ordination of ministers.

Experiences and Practices

To collate and measure the Pentecostal experiences and practices of pastors fifteen items were combined to form an *Experiences and Practices (EXPRA) Scale*. Analysis of the frequencies provides evidence of the contemporary

---

43. Poloma, "Assemblies of God at the Crossroads," 179, 209.

44. See Kerr, "Revised Report," 1–3. The AoG's statistics indicated the average size church was 168, 59% of all AoG churches were less than 100, while 3.74% were over 500, with only 1.93% over 1000.

importance for pastors of Pentecostal experiences. The approach taken was to assume these to be normal human responses to the perception of the divine. All are indicators of a personal relationship with God (although not all are distinctly Pentecostal). Praying in tongues (glossolalia) is an experience central to Pentecostal beliefs. It has been defined as prayer focused directly to God generally in a humanly unintelligible language. As a paranormal experience it is viewed as normative within Pentecostalism. Most Pentecostal attenders would support the view that glossolalia is a supernatural gift, although subject to the speaker's control, which gives an ability to speak in an unknown but genuine language intended for the purpose of prayer.[45] For Pentecostals, "tongues is normative for their experience, just as it was normative in the experience of the apostolic churches recorded in Acts."[46]

Prophecy may be defined as a gift of the Spirit by which a person speaks in the name of God giving an exhortation, encouragement, reporting a vision, providing illumination or interpreting a message in tongues. It may be given in a public church service or as a personal prophecy privately to an individual. It may involve what the person believes are specific directions or guidance from God or personal confirmation of biblical truths. The experience of "falling under the power," also called "being slain in the Spirit" or "resting in the Spirit," occurs when a person falls, often backwards, when one or more people "lay hands" on the person in prayer—this is also attributed to the power of the Holy Spirit. Some practices, such as receiving answers to prayer or "feeling led" by God to perform a specific action, are not distinctively Pentecostal, but they share common features closely related to Pentecostal experience and nurture their manifestation.

Significantly, *all* of the pastors who responded to the question about praying in tongues indicated they had done so regularly. Ninety-two percent indicated they "received a definite answer" when they had prayed. As seen previously, early Pentecostal spirituality was characterized by strong emphasis on praying in tongues.

However, when it came to having "given a public prophecy in church," fewer pastors (64%) indicated they had done this. Thirty-four percent had done so only occasionally. Even less (43%) indicated they had "given a prophecy privately to another person." Forty-seven percent had "occasionally." The variance of public prophecy compared to private praying

---

45. Poloma, "*Assemblies of God at the Crossroads*," 27–28, 36–38.

46. Stronstad, *Charismatic Theology of St. Luke*, 16. See Macchia's treatment of the significance of tongues, in "Struggle for Global Witness," 8–29.

in tongues is considered in Poloma's study, which showed the relative openness of pastors to the manifestation of prophecy to have institutional ramifications. Prophecy is seen as gift for the church in general and not simply personal spiritual experience. More than Spirit baptism and glossolalia, these "paranormal leadings can be institutionally dangerous" and cause serious problems of order in a service. This causes some pastors to be wary of some Pentecostal expressions in public with the result that they may attempt to keep a lid on expressions that have given Pentecostalism its distinctiveness.[47]

Sixty percent of the pastors reported they have "felt led" by God to perform a specific action. Less than 13% had "fallen under the power of the Spirit." Only 10% indicated they had "expressed holy laughter." However, 69% had "heard God speak by personal confirmation of scripture." A mere 14% testify to having often "received a miraculous healing" (but 60% occasionally). Only 15% have often "heard God speak through a vision or dream," 54% have occasionally, but 27% hardly ever, and 4% never. Only 3% indicated often experiencing "a demonic deliverance," although 33% had occasionally, 44% hardly ever have, and 20% never.[48] In contrast, accounts of early Pentecostal spirituality including in the AoG had reasonably frequent references to deliverance ministry.

With regard to more general spiritual experiences a high 94% indicated they have "had a deep sense of God's presence." Sixty-six percent indicated they have "had a personal encounter with God." By contrast, only 10% of pastors often had a personal experience of having "given a message in tongues in church," but 41% indicated they had occasionally, with a significant 38% hardly ever, and 11% never. By contrast, the reflections of the older key AoG ministers as discussed later, recall regular messages in tongues in earlier Pentecostal services. Finally, only 29% had "danced with joy before the Lord."

The results of the *Experiences and Practices (EXPRA)* above show a varied picture. Some individual experiences, like praying in tongues had high frequency scores. However, the *EPRA* Index measuring all the responses in this category reveals an overall average of only 45% (of either "frequently" or "quite often"). Experiences such as: giving a prophecy

47. Poloma, *Assemblies of God at the Crossroads*, 77.

48. The figures on this question may be skewed by variations in interpretation as to whether the question is asking if the pastor personally received deliverance or was involved in ministering deliverance to someone. In either case, they seem to indicate that a substantial number of pastors have limited experience in this area.

privately to another person, falling under the power, holy laughter, receiving miraculous healing, hearing God speak through a vision or dream, experiencing a demonic deliverance, giving a message in tongues in church and dancing with joy before the Lord, all have lower than the index's average frequencies. Practices that are more frequent and well above 50% were: praying in tongues, receiving a definite answer to prayer, giving a prophecy in church, feeling led by God to perform a specific action, hearing God speak by personal confirmation of scripture, having a deep sense of God's presence and having a personal encounter with God. It appears less than half of the practices in this index have reasonably strong frequencies for pastors but more than half are less than average in frequency. Although not all these practices were clearly identified as part of early Pentecostal spirituality, arguably most are. When integrated with other qualitative information, the indication is that Pentecostal pastors in the AoG are moving away from a number of key Pentecostal practices that form a major part of early classical Pentecostal spirituality.

Private Devotional Practices

Nine specific questions focused on the pastors' own private devotional practices as part of the expression of their spirituality. These were measured by the frequency of spending time in certain activities and combined into a single *PRIDEV* index of Private Devotional Practices. These could not be termed exclusively Pentecostal practices. Ninety-eight percent of the pastors who responded indicated they had spent significant time in "private Bible reading." Ninety-four percent spent time in "intentional private prayer." Eighty-eight percent spent time in "biblical meditation." Sixty-four percent indicated they "read devotional literature." Sixty-seven percent "made use of tapes, CDs, DVDs or videos." With regard to fasting, 22% responded they did so regularly and 59% did so occasionally. Nevertheless, 19% hardly ever fast and 1% never have. Pastors taking time to go "on a prayer retreat" is an area of concern. Only 6% go at least quite often, 42% indicate they go occasionally, and it may be a concern that 42% admit they hardly ever go, with 11% indicating they never do. Sixty percent indicated they often "made time to reflect on their life and directions." A significant number indicated they do so only occasionally (37%) or hardly ever (4%). Journaling was not that popular with only 36% indicating they "kept a personal devotional journal."

The *PRIVDEV* Index of measured an average figure of 59% of the overall responses to "frequently" and "quite often" in this category. The areas that indicated low scores (under 50%) and may need improvement are biblical fasting, going on a prayer retreat and keeping a prayer journal. Areas that showed scores higher than 50% were time spent in private Bible reading, intentional prayer, biblical meditation, reading devotional literature and making time to reflect on life and directions. It must be conceded that areas like journaling and reflecting on life and directions have no available historical data for comparison and so our information provides an impressionistic view of any development. These practices are generally regarded as widely accepted aspects of Christian spirituality and the frequencies in the index may be indicating a trend toward more mainline practices. Certainly, there appears to be a focus on the more activist practices than the more reflective practices and forms. The challenge here may be for the pastors to integrate both aspects in their lives.

Church Services and Practices

This category (CHSERV) sought to measure the frequency of various Pentecostal practices within the pastors' churches. "Tongues and interpretation" may be seen as a particular manifestation or one form of "prophecy." One person speaks aloud in tongues in a service and another delivers the "interpretation" in a known human language. The glossolalic message is an indication that God has a prophetic word for the congregation. Silence follows while the congregation waits for someone to interpret. The more common form of prophecy is where a person may simply deliver a prophetic word (without waiting for a glossolalic utterance to come from another member). Glossolalia may also be used as a means of corporate praise and worship where people pray or sing aloud in tongues while others at the same time pray or sing in English. This requires no interpretation as it is viewed as simply an acceptable congregational prayer or worship form. Some Pentecostals are embarrassed by manifestations such as "falling under the power" and question whether they are truly of the "Spirit' or the "flesh." Some believe it is genuine, but usually due to high suggestibility. "Dancing in the Spirit" usually refers to spontaneous dancing by the congregation mostly in the same spot (and without partners) and is viewed as a biblical part of corporate worship like praying or singing together. Old line classical Pentecostals see dancing in the Spirit as something that occurs when the

Spirit takes over a person, leading them to dance in a more trancelike state and they often regard the "charismatic" form of dancing as really only done "in the flesh."

Only 22% of pastors indicated that "tongues and interpretation" were practiced regularly in their church. A significant 51% said it was only occasional but a considerable 24% hardly ever and 3% never. This appears to be in contrast to accounts given by older AoG ministers of early Pentecostal church services where messages in "tongues and interpretation" were a regular feature of church life. "Prophecies" fared better with 58% saying they often took place in their church services, 37% occasionally and 5% hardly ever. "Singing in the Spirit" had a significant 71% indicating this took place often. "Praying in tongues" was similar with 70% saying it occurred regularly in their church with 25% affirming it occurred only occasionally and 5% hardly ever.

Forty-seven percent indicated "testimonies of miracles" often occurred in their church services and 48% occasionally. "Testimonies of divine healing" were a little less, with 40% indicating they often occurred and 54% occasionally. Forty-one percent of pastors said "testimonies of personal salvation" often occurred in their church services. A low 25% indicated that "dancing in the Spirit" often occurred in their church. For "falling under the power of the Spirit," 34% of pastors indicated this often happened in their church (48% only occasionally).

With regard to "altar calls/prayer for baptism in the Holy Spirit," 59% indicated this regularly occurred in their church, 38% said it happened occasionally and 4% said it hardly ever occurred. This seems to indicate a significant support for the experience of the classical AoG doctrine of the baptism of the Holy Spirit. All 106 respondents to question 35 indicated that "altar calls/prayer for healing" occurred in their church (90% often and 10% occasionally). The results show respondents supporting AoG Pentecostal doctrine and belief that healing is a normal experience. Eighty-two percent of respondents indicated "altar calls/prayer for salvation" occurred.

The *CHSERV* Index in relation to *Church Services and Practices* measured twelve items of ritual in AoG services. The overall average of either "frequently" or "quite often" in this category was 53%. Areas that indicated frequencies below average for this Index that may be of concern were: tongues and interpretation, testimonies of miracles, of divine healing and of personal salvation, dancing in the Spirit, and falling under the power of the Spirit. Areas above 50% were prophecies, singing in the Spirit, altar calls/prayer for the baptism in the Holy Spirit, healing and salvation and praying in tongues. Overall the Index appears to show change away from the regular occurrences of these practices of Pentecostal spirituality in AoG church services.

Community Service and Outreach

This category sought to measure the aspect of spirituality that relates to outward mission and service. Sixty percent of pastors regularly speak "to a non-church person about Christ," 38% do so occasionally, and 2% hardly ever. Over half the pastors had often "prayed for a specific person to receive Christ"; for a significant 45% this occurs only occasionally with it hardly ever for 10%. Often "inviting a non-church person to church," scored a little lower at 45%. Those who often served "in a church outreach or community welfare program" were again well over half (57%). Those who often "served in a community service, social action or welfare not connected to the church," was significantly low at 20%, (with 28% occasionally, a large 40% hardly ever have, and 13% never).

The *COMOUT* Index for this section measured the above five items, which came to an average of 48%. Three items in this index measured over 50%. Two items were well below 50%: inviting a non-church person to a church service and for serving in a community service or social action or welfare unconnected with the church. Apart from information on the Good News Hall in the Depression years there is not much data on early Pentecostal social outreach ministry. With the lack of record in Pentecostal publications and other accounts, one could reasonably infer that social welfare ministry was not a strong aspect of early AoG (Pentecostal) spirituality. Data from the views of the key AoG ministers presented later show a mixed picture but generally indicates more involvement by pastors in these areas than previously.

Beliefs and Attitudes

Questions 44–50 deal with the beliefs and attitudes of AoG pastors, as a measure of their Pentecostal spirituality. A high 97% of pastors agreed with the statement, "in general I feel very positive about my church," a low 3% were neutral or unsure and only one respondent disagreed with the statement. Again a high 94% agreed that in general they felt "very positive about being a pastor," only 4% neutral or unsure and one respondent disagreeing. Almost all the respondents agreed with the statement that "over the past year I have grown in my faith," with only one respondent neutral or unsure.

The *BEATT* index, as an average of the total items, measured 69%. If question 46, in relation to baptism in the Holy Spirit being able to be experienced without tongues, was taken out of the equation, the index would measure a high 77%. Four items specifically dealt with baptism in the Holy Spirit and "the tongues issue." As discussed previously, Spirit baptism is understood by classical Pentecostals to be a work of the Spirit distinct from and usually subsequent to conversion and the sign or tangible evidence is speaking in tongues.[49] The survey looked at pastors' beliefs and attitudes about the statement that the "baptism in the Holy Spirit may be experienced without tongues." Four percent strongly agreed and 16% agreed, with 20% neutral or unsure about this, indicating that 40% of senior pastors appear to be unsure or neutral about a cardinal doctrinal belief of the AoG. Only 60% of pastors either disagreed (35%) or strongly disagreed (25%) with the statement. This is despite the fact that AoG pastors must have this experience of speaking in tongues before being ordained. Of the 135 pastors who responded to question 50, that "speaking in tongues is necessary as evidence of Spirit Baptism," 77% either strongly agreed (30%) or agreed (47%), with 13% neutral or unsure, 10% disagreed, with only one respondent strongly disagreeing. Again, it appears nearly one quarter (24%) have some uncertainty or disagreement with the denominational doctrinal position.

The difference between the responses may indicate that some pastors, particularly those from neo-Pentecostal backgrounds, are doing their own reinterpretation of "initial evidence" in Article 5:13 of the United Constitution of the AoG National General Conference and/or they may be simply reiterating the accepted doctrinal position.

Seventy-five percent of pastors either strongly agreed (26%) or agreed (49%) that "speaking in tongues should be a requirement for leadership in the church," 12% were neutral or unsure, 11% disagreed and 2% strongly disagreed. However, only 5% strongly agreed and 16% agreed that "speaking in tongues should be a requirement for church membership/partnership." Nearly 80% of the 120 pastors who responded to this would probably

---

49. See Poloma's sociological research into glossolalia, "Assemblies of God at the Crossroads," 34–40, and Chant on sociological findings on glossolalia as applied to Australian Pentecostalism in *Spirit of Pentecost*, 83–98.

not insist it be a requirement for membership (19% were neutral or unsure, 48% disagreed with 31% strongly disagreeing).

A Mixed Picture

In previous chapters we have seen how important *experience* is in the birthing, development and renewal of Pentecostal spirituality as a form of Christian spirituality. Data collected from AoG pastors in Australia show that experiences of the presence of the Spirit of God are still important today but there appears to be some developmental change in their spirituality with a varied picture emerging.

Low frequencies in some of the classical Pentecostal practices appear to indicate a lessening in some of the oral, narrative and participatory liturgies. This could be expected, partly because of an increasingly literary society and the continual influence of Evangelical theology. There also appears to be a change of emphasis with regards to experiencing the immanent presence of the Spirit of God with a movement from the more classical spiritual expressions such as messages in tongues or prophecy by individuals, to more corporate and controlled spiritual expressions, such as combined singing in the Spirit and community praise and worship in church services.

The emphasis on altar calls for healing and baptism in the Spirit seem as strong as ever but there is a decline in the exercise of spiritual gifts such as public messages in tongues and prophecy or visions and dreams, which may be problematic to the church as an institution. The increase in congregational sizes may also make the exercise of these gifts difficult. Despite this, these pastors in Australia still appear to be emphasizing the importance of affective action within an organization that has come out of humble beginnings to one that is institutionally modern and reaching the middle class.[50] In the next chapter the place of institutionalization in this change in the pastors Pentecostal spirituality is considered in depth.

---

50. One of the problematic issues with regard to this data from the national survey is the response rate of 22.35%; 135 out of 604 pastors responded to the survey. One must therefore be tentative about drawing conclusions based on the survey data alone. However, the survey results were not relied on in isolation but integrated with the information from the key ministers and the author's observations over many years.

5

Assessing the Results

Introduction

AT THE BEGINNING WE established that Christian "spirituality" was a descriptive term for the work of the Holy Spirit in living the Christian life. It relates mainly to the interior dimension but cannot be separated from its outworking in the external world. In the second chapter we surveyed the background of the Pentecostal/Charismatic movement, which revealed its spirituality had a unique emphasis on the initiative and work of the Holy Spirit in the believer. Pentecostal theology on "the second blessing" impacts on Pentecostal spirituality, and conversely its spirituality informs on Pentecostal/Charismatic theology. Pentecostal spirituality could not be restricted to Pentecostal theology and required empirical observation. In chapter three it was shown that considerable consistency could be seen in what are the essential features of classical Pentecostal spirituality (including the AoG). The importance of personal *experience* of the Spirit was found to be paramount.

In more recent years the influence of the Charismatic renewal and the neo-Pentecostal movements, have impacted on Pentecostal denominations and movements. In particular, AoG pastors seem to be no longer confining themselves to the classical doctrinal position in current practice, particularly with regard to Spirit baptism and glossolalia. They are more concerned with the *experience* of the working of the Holy Spirit and the *exercise* of spiritual gifts rather than holding to the classical formal theological position on "initial evidence," "consequence" and "subsequence." Some might argue these pastors are being more consistently "truly Pentecostal" in refusing to be constrained to written doctrinal creeds and theologies, even though they were enshrined by their own Pentecostal forefathers in the early decades of the twentieth century.

Data collected from senior pastors and key ministers in Australia show that there does appear to be a move away from an emphasis on individual crisis-type experience of Spirit baptism and from classical expressions of spirituality to those that are more corporate and controlled.

Reflections of Key Ministers

Key ministers, who agreed to reflect on the survey's results and on Pentecostal spirituality in general, confirmed that the data supported their beliefs that there had been a drift in the practices of Pentecostal spirituality by the pastors, summarized as follows: They thought AoG pastors were "drift[ing] away from disciplined Pentecostal practices." Pastors seemed "stronger in the ministry of the Word of God" and "weaker on the gifts of the Spirit." One minister described the pastors as being moderate or "centre of the road when it comes to experiencing realities of the Spirit's presence." It was generally thought that AoG pastors' passion for Pentecostal experiences needed to increase otherwise there was danger that "conservative approaches to the supernatural may creep in." Although AoG pastors appeared to be consistently involved in "Pentecostal practices" in their own personal spiritual life, there was a decrease in their public practices. It was also suggested that pastors nowadays were less "dogmatic" on what was considered to be "non-essential doctrinal positions." However, positions taken on matters like glossolalia, for example, go to the very heart of the identity of the Pentecostal movement. One minister was unconvinced by the high frequencies for this category and actually expected the results to be lower. He was encouraged to see many pastors at least "occasionally" experiencing Pentecostal phenomena. But he surmised if this reflected "too few" numbers then the movement has a problem.[1]

These ministers believe the results showed that most pastors still prayed in tongues and prophesied despite the increase in "the seeker friendly nature of many churches and the change in emphasis in many public services." One Executive minister in the 40–50 age group said the low results for personal prophecy may be because many pastors are becoming

---

1. Case 32, Cettolin, "AOG Pentecostal Spirituality in Australia."

very "leadership focused" and as a result are sharing "the latest books or fads with each other rather than God's prompting." Concern was expressed that over 40% of pastors who indicated they were "only occasionally" or "never" led by the Spirit. It was surmised that responses to questions about operation of spiritual gifts would have been higher if asked during the 1990s when there was a greater emphasis on the "Toronto Blessing," "Rodney Howard Browne's Ministry" and the "Pensacola revival."

During the 1960s and 1970s, there invariably were public messages in tongues in church services, usually by a pastor or a regular public tongues-speaker. Nowadays, almost half the pastors have *never* given a public message in tongues. This is probably due to a change in perspective by pastors that tongues are for believers and that the practice alienates non-Christian "seekers." One minister has never heard a message in tongues in *any* public service in the last five years.

Several of the ministers were more "optimistic" about the results stating that they indicated senior pastors were "committed to experiencing God." The results were interpreted as being encouraging, as they reflected "a balance" in pastors' lives with "Pentecostal distinctives" characterizing their ministries. They also indicated a high level of maturity in pastors who have "a well rounded view of spirituality" and are "are sincere, devout, godly and spiritual." One State Executive member found the results encouraging but a marked contrast to NCLS research that showed many ministers struggling and wanting to leave the ministry. Despite the fact that many pastors were using "seeker-sensitive" approaches in their church meetings, the results showed "a healthy desire for the moving of the Spirit." Even though the results for AoG pastors' spiritual experiences were higher than generally anticipated, it was believed they still needed "to press in deeper, experiencing greater levels of Holy Ghost anointing."

Changes in AoG (Pentecostal) Spirituality

Despite the limitations of the survey's response rate and its design, the data from the key ministers views when integrated together with the results data show changes and development in classical Pentecostal beliefs, changes in demonstrable Pentecostal practices in church services and also changes in the pastors' own beliefs about the importance of these expressions.

Most of the key ministers thought that: Pentecostal spirituality in the AoG was changing with some detrimental results. Rather than holding to the classical Pentecostal view on tongues, AoG pastors are adopting a more "Third Wave" position (those who hold to the validity of the gifts of the Spirit but do not require a climactic second blessing experience, evidenced by speaking in tongues) or a more "Charismatic" position.[2] Classical Pentecostals from AoG churches claim the normative pattern of Spirit baptism as a distinct and separate experience that follows salvation with speaking in tongues as the "initial evidence." Most AoG senior pastors are now content in practice, if not in formal statement of belief, for church members to acknowledge the gifts of the Spirit including tongues, without pressing the need for a crisis-type baptism of the Spirit after conversion.

Only a few ministers believed that their movement's Pentecostal spirituality "is changing without any visible negative results." Even so, they still acknowledged that there was some change, and that the pastors needed to embrace a fresh supernatural experience if the AoG movement is to continue in its present rate of growth. One admitted there was a broadening of attitudes and practices with a decline in emphasis on "tongues and interpretation" in church services. A small number believed that the changes merely reflected stylistic developments in public meetings but the fundamental practices were virtually the same. One minister said there was minor change due to "seeker-sensitive approaches" but not to belief in essential AoG doctrine. Another did not think AoG spirituality was changing and was "reasonably surprised to see that Pentecostal spirituality is strong in the sample with the ministers and their churches." Yet another, that there was "more balanced" spirituality than in the past but it was crucial that it not "swing too much the other way." It was important that AoG churches were contemporary in style and that rather than doing away with Pentecostal experiences, fresh and modern expressions were needed. One minister thought that Pentecostal spirituality was "healthier" than in the past. "We are looking now to a more natural use of the gifts in the market place of everyday life and not just after two slow songs in a Sunday morning service."

The key senior ministers in the older age categories (60–70 years and the 70–80 years) generally expressed that there had been a drift from early AoG Pentecostal heritage, practices and stated classical doctrinal beliefs. Some believed this was due to the influence of the Charismatic renewal.

---

2. The term now used recently for those who hold to the validity and use of the gifts of the Spirit but do not mandate the requirement of speaking in tongues to validate their experience of the Spirit.

They thought it was clear some pastors have not had a radical crisis-type experience of the baptism of the Holy Spirit. One minister said:

> There appears to be less emphasis on the Baptism of the Spirit than in early years. Speaking in tongues is still a high value but as the "evidence" it is not regarded across the board with the emphatic view of yesteryear . . . the results appear to show a broadening of attitudes and practices and a declining emphasis on "tongues and interpretation" in public services.

Another in the 70–80 age group who was converted in the 1930s and began ministry in the 1940s, commented that "holiness was a significant distinctive of early Pentecostalism" in contrast to today. In his view, "tongues speaking should be seen, heard and known in an authentic Pentecostal church" and this was an area of "decline or diminishment of Pentecostal distinctives."

Conclusions

There appears to be less emphasis on Pentecostal/charismatic experiences and practices as classically expressed. Pastors appear to be also frequently using mainline (non-Pentecostal) forms in their private devotional practices. Clearly there is a move toward decrease in classical Pentecostal practices in church services but a growing involvement in community services and outreach. Movement away from classical Pentecostal beliefs and attitudes are being shown and increasingly "Charismatic" and "Third Wave" beliefs and approaches are being adopted. Taking all the data into account together, there seems to be a convergence of evidence that indicates the hypothesis to be tenable—that Pentecostal spirituality is changing for AoG pastors and churches. There are limitations on these conclusions. The data from the survey results was derived from late 2004 and there will have been subsequent developments since then. Although it is difficult to generalize too widely about the reasons or causes of the change in AoG (Pentecostal) spirituality, some reasoned reflections and speculations are given in the next chapter.

6

Reflections

Sociological Insights

PENTECOSTALISM WAS BIRTHED IN distinctive experiences of the presence and power of the Spirit, challenging the more formal and clergy-dominated concept of the church. Although other movements have done this throughout history, Pentecostalism was unique in that it called for the release of the laity in the "priesthood of all believers" in practice, not only in doctrine. It opened the possibility of the prophetic gifts for all who were Spirit-filled in a "democratization" of ministry. It proclaimed that the spiritual gifts were available to all believers who earnestly sought the Holy Spirit. To protect these experiences the early Pentecostals resisted formal structures especially those set up by ordination. Over later years and more in recent years, this approach is being replaced by the development of more formal and structured patterns of leadership.

This development and perspective is mirrored by the early sociologist Max Weber's thesis. He argued this type of development took place in all kinds of groups and organizations, described in sociological terms as *routinization* or *institutionalization*. Confusion came when Weber and others used the key biblical word "charisma" as a purely sociological term. For Weber "charismatic" leadership is leadership offered by someone of extraordinary personal power and ability, who others willingly follow. "Charisma" was seen as latent human qualities in extraordinary leaders. Weber's insights are helpful, however, to illustrate what we have observed in this study.

REFLECTIONS

Although institutionalization is a process recognized by students of sociological trends, as a Christian minister and researcher my predominant concern is a moving away from the freedom and work of the Holy Spirit in the church. Most Christians comprehend "charisma" in theological terms to mean the spiritual gifts given by the Spirit of God, which may be received by all God's people. Although Weber correctly recognized that routinization and organization often follow breakthrough brought about by a "charismatic" leader, he was incorrect to think that such developments always destroy this charisma. In theological terms, the Spirit of God through the "charisma," sometimes is actually responsible for the innovative creation of structures and forms to ensure the organization's own survival.

What makes Pentecostal pastors and churches different from Evangelicals is the acceptance of paranormal experiences from the Spirit of God as normative. However, Pentecostal pastors have also found it necessary to avoid the chaos resulting from an unrestrained freedom of the human element that have characterized some Pentecostal meetings and the extremism that would make institutional stability impossible. In my view, pastors are an important key to creating an orderly setting in which Pentecostal type experiences may still occur. Pentecostal rituals in churches provide these opportunities. It is the local pastor empowered by the Spirit of God who is in a unique influential position to encourage charisma or alternatively to put more structure in place, as appropriate.

Institutionalization

Although growth and change in individuals is taken for granted, we are less familiar with ageing in organizations. Nevertheless, the social sciences have observed and documented a process of group development that begins with human interaction and continues as long as the group exists. This process of "institutionalization," refers to a pattern of change by which spontaneous, living movements become rigid, structured and inflexible. The activities, values, experiences and relationships of the group become formalized and stabilized so that predictable behavior and rigid organizational structures emerge. "The seeds of organizational decay begin to flower as the movement passes beyond its original phase and as a second generation takes over leadership."[1] Eddie Gibbs expresses this process as the way religious

1. Tidball, *Introduction to the Sociology of the New Testament*, 123–26.

groups develop from *men* to *movements*, turn into *machines* and eventually become *monuments*.[2]

Nevertheless, movements cannot function without some structure. Total freedom from structure is not possible or even desirable. The problem lies with the detrimental aspects of institutionalization which commence when structures cease to function in the best interests of the movement they are meant to serve. Many start out as a vigorous movement or sect, but as the second generation takes over with growth and complexity, they become less dynamic and free.[3] They become "routinized" because daily life cannot function very long on the unpredictable, needing a certain amount of stability.

One analysis put forward on the basis of organizational theory and close observation of churches is that of David Moberg. He postulated a "process of institutionalization" framework for church development in five stages that eventually ends in decline. In the early days the *incipient organization* has few structures and strong leadership; a *formal organization* eventually develops where the leadership imposes greater cohesion, then; *maximum efficiency* operates with less emotionalism and more stability, next; bureaucracy and leadership develop in the *institutional phase* to where it perpetuates its own interests—there is little spontaneity in worship and belief becomes a creedal vestige from the past. The church no longer sees itself as distinct to outsiders and toleration rules; uncorrected this leads to the fifth stage of *disintegration or decline*. This "institutionalization" process is general and not only limited to the fourth stage. The activities, values, experiences and relationships of the group become formalized and established so that predictable behavior and rigid organizational structures emerge.[4] Interestingly, Menzies believed Moberg denied ultimate deterioration is inevitable once "maximum efficiency" is reached and that "internal reform may reverse the process." He concluded the AG in America was "near the optimum in the balance between spiritual vitality and efficient organization."[5]

---

2. Gibbs, *Body-Building Exercises*, 24.

3. The words "sect" and "denomination" are used technically in the sociological sense. A sect can become institutionalized without ceasing to be a sect; a denomination may be more or less institutionalized.

4. Moberg, *Church as a Social Institution*, 22, 118–24.

5. Menzies, *Anointed to Serve*, 382.

Thomas O'Dea analyzed Moberg's components and he identified five dilemmas every religious institution faces and finds impossible to escape. He elaborated Weber's classic theory of "charisma" and saw an inherent institutionalization in religion. He saw a fundamental tension that stems from the fact that "religion desperately needs institutionalization yet suffers much from it." He describes the problem in terms of a compromise between *spontaneity* and *stability*, referred to as the "routinization of charisma." If "charisma" is to endure over time in modern society it will be "bureaucratized" in some form.[6] It would be critical to many in the Pentecostal movement that its bureaucracy serves and nurtures the original spirit and not lead to an organization that uses or controls the experience of the Spirit to further itself, resulting in the charisma being overpowered by rationality, pragmatism and efficiency.

Institutional Dilemmas

The five dilemmas are: First, *mixed motivation*: a single-minded leader does not deviate from the clear mission but subsequent leaders start to work for other reasons. Second, *symbolic dilemma*: originally, worship is a person's response to the transcendent, but for it to be repeated, the sacred is symbolically enshrined in words, objects and actions which makes it mundane. Survival demands established forms. The worshipper begins to respond to external routine ritual instead of the sacred and true worship no longer takes place. Third, *administrative order*: bureaucratic structure is enlarged to handle problems but is never dismantled, becoming a hindrance. Fourth, *delimitation*: insights of charismatic leaders become stereotyped so followers know what the acceptable orthodoxy is. Doctrine gets rigidly defined and instead of the Spirit giving life, the written code kills. Fifth, *power*: originally people join a movement through conversion. The first step away is when children of the converts join who are socialized into the movement. Growth and popularity further lessen the demands of membership. Finally, a movement becomes so widely accepted that it becomes allied to the wider culture.[7]

Putting O'Dea's thesis simply, movements are institutionalizing when they experience a "fragmentation of goals"; a "mixing of the leader's motives"; a "formalization of worship"; an uncontrolled "mushrooming

6. O'Dea, "Five Dilemmas," 30–41.
7. Ibid.

of bureaucracy"; a "petrifying of definitions" and a "pursuit of power or popularity."[8] In sociological terms, if these five institutional dilemmas appear to be alive it would indicate a strong co-presence of "charisma" within the institution.

Maraget Poloma in North America found that, despite its large organization, the AG was still experiencing vitality and growth due to its ability to encourage personal participation in the charisma without jeopardizing its organizational structure, action actually viewed as indicative of the work of the Holy Spirit.[9] Nevertheless, despite its organizational success, the AG still struggled against those very forces of success quenching personal leadings by the Spirit. Sociologically, religious experiences are often deemed to be "dangerous" in that charismatic prophets who hear from God tend to threaten the institutional order; dangers that are often reduced and routinized by means of "institutionalization."[10]

In Australia, the very success of the AoG and the inevitable growth of its bureaucratic structure has produced certain tensions and faces the threat of over-institutionalization and over-regulation, which has the tendency to quench the Holy Spirit and the working of the spiritual gifts. The findings and observations on the AoG will be compared and contrasted with Poloma's landmark research work.

Mixed Motivation

As one example of the existence of the dilemma of *mixed motivation* is the exclusion of women from leadership positions. As a gauge it measures the rise of professional clergy that jeopardizes the priesthood of all believers. In North America the AG has allowed its success as an institution to block avenues once open to women. The original enthusiasm of early Pentecostalism that recognized charisma rather than social status, gives way to a priestly clergy that draws a distinction between the leaders and the led.[11] Jacqueline Grey finds this dilemma demonstrated in the AoG in Australia,

---

8. Tidball, *Social Context*, 125–28.

9. Poloma, *Assemblies of God*, 5. Poloma analyzed data from 1275 AG adherents in 16 congregations and 246 ministers and sought to show the importance of religious experiences in the construction of Pentecostal/Charismatic reality.

10. Ibid., 11, 207–8.

11. Ibid., 120–21, 208.

where she says the development of the ministry has become a *profession* rather than charismatic *gifting*:

> The routinisation of charisma has produced a new professional clergy that undermines the values of charismatic leadership: the very tradition on which the fellowship was founded. The dilemma of "mixed motivation" is expressed in the tension between the *satisfaction* received by, on the one hand, office and prestige, and the values of charisma gifting on the other.[12]

Although opportunities appear to be improving for women ministers in the AoG, there are still limitations when it comes to positions of power such as senior pastorates or executive positions at state and national level. The *Report on Women Holding Credentials in the Assemblies of God* states that of 935 senior pastors in the AoG in Australia as of September 2002, 33 or just 4% are women and only 13.58% of all ordained ministers (OMC) are women, that is 158. This is a far cry from the early Australian Pentecostalism where half the congregations by 1930 were established and led by women. The more encouraging statistic was that 193, that is 37.2% of probationary minister credentials (PMC), were held by women.[13] Well over a decade later the picture shows significant increase in overall numbers but little seems to have changed with regard to senior positions. Figures from 2014 *ACC Census* data and the *ACC Database* September 2015 reveal that 992 of the total number of 3,224 leaders with a credential (both OMCs and PMCs) are women, that is, 30.7%. However, what is not clear is whether they hold an OMC or PMC. What is clear is that females represent 57% of church attenders and 51% of ACC church staff.[14]

ACC National Executive member Donna Crouch writes, while "women are functioning effectively at a local church level" they are not yet occupying "senior areas of responsibility, such as church planting, senior pastors, board members and chairperson positions." Although there has been some increase in District, State and National Executive roles and some women church planters, "however, it is still an anomaly—and certainly not reflective of how many women ministers [are] credentialed."[15]

12. Grey, "Prophetic (M)others," 48–49.
13. Kerr, "Revised Report," 1–2, 27–28.
14. *ACC EMag*, 18.
15. Crouch, "Leadership Pipeline," 18.

Administrative Order

Poloma found that despite early protests from the Pentecostal pioneers, an elaborate organization emerged in the AG denomination in North America, and it grew often at the expense of the freedom of the Spirit. Prophets without a congregational power base were easily silenced but they could still find a forum in local congregations led by highly charismatic ministers. The dilemma remained viable because of the relative autonomy of the individual churches.[16] In contrast to the AG's centralized executive structure, in Australia, the National and State Executive leaders who continue to pastor their own often large and autonomous, churches fill the positions. These leaders are free within the AoG to carry out ministries that have contributed to growth and success of the movement. As a result the Australian structure remained sufficiently flexible to allow for the continued experience of the presence of the Spirit and the working of the gifts. Nevertheless, these "charismatic" voices are always under threat of being overwhelmed by the accommodative forces of an instant-results culture, human models of church growth and success, pragmatism, efficiency, wealth, power, fashion, entertainment, lifestyle and the appeal of political power.

Symbolic Dilemma

The *symbolic dilemma* is demonstrated where experiences of the Spirit of God in Pentecostal/Charismatic ritual are replaced by routine liturgical forms. Pentecostals have their own rites or rituals (meaningful symbolic acts) such as the laying on of hands, speaking in tongues, raising hands in worship and so forth. Ritual more than any other factor, encourages or discourages openness to Pentecostal experience basic to Pentecostal spirituality and distinctiveness. "Paradoxically . . . symbols, rituals, ceremonies can be easily concretized in the institutionalization process, making them barriers instead of helps in transmitting the very religious experiences that may have generated them."[17] Worship becomes less a person's response to God and a more mundane response to an external form. This dilemma is the most important but the most difficult for keeping charisma alive where forces of institutionalization and accommodation work against it. Poloma's study found that highly experiential pastors lead more charismatic church-

---

16. Poloma, *Assemblies of God at the Crossroads*, 209.
17. Ibid., xviii, 11.

es so that the members share the charismata, the experience of the Spirit and the practice of the spiritual gifts.[18]

My observations made in the last thirty-seven years in Australia indicate that, apart from short seasons influenced by the "Pensacola revival," "Rodney Howard Brown Ministries" or the "Toronto Blessing," and now the "Bethel" movement the spontaneity of many services have became noticeably less. This is particularly so as churches became larger and their demographics have changed. As Pentecostal churches became more urbane, there was an increasing demand for more structured services, professional production, skilled musicianship and sophistication of church services. Despite this, Pentecostal services are still less formal than the usual non-Pentecostal or Evangelical service. Most pastors promote the reality of a Pentecostal worldview that teaches the normality of spiritual experiences. God is not seen to be distant but personally involved with his people. Most AoG pastors in the survey, as confirmed by the key ministers, indicated they prayed in tongues frequently, experienced definite answers to prayer, have been led to perform certain acts, experienced healing, have heard God speak in Scripture, have had a deep sense of his presence and have had a personal encounter with God.

Although AoG churches generally now use contemporary-styled music (usually Hillsong music or their own songs), their worship services differ from most other non-Pentecostal churches. They involve some congregational participation, emphasis on "praise and worship" music and singing and at times, spontaneity. Worship styles and approaches do vary from church to church. In some it is loud and celebrative and seemingly spontaneous while in others it is short and routine, yet in both the experience of God's immanent presence in church services still occurs.

Generally however, Pentecostal experiences of the Spirit are changing from less individually expressed phenomena to more orchestrated corporate manifestations. Church congregations now mainly experience the presence of the Spirit of God through corporate worship, and short times of coordinated charismatic expression such as combined free worship and singing in the Spirit. This is in contrast to the more individualized expressions of past years such as tongues and interpretation or prophecy.

It may be that changes in personal Pentecostal experiences and practices by pastors are being reflected in the church services. Pentecostal ritual officially promotes classical Pentecostal doctrine, but the data indicates that

---

18. Ibid., 185–86, 211.

individual expressions of tongues and interpretation and prophecies from ordinary members are becoming less frequent in church services. This is despite the fact that pastors are claiming to regularly pray in tongues in private.

Pastors may be more sensitive to the possibility of "fleshly," overly emotional or disorderly practices by individuals in the congregational setting or they may be concerned that the gifts will be abused or misused. In the late 1970s and 1980s, I observed a number of instances of inappropriate or immature use of the prophetic gifts, sometimes to indirectly "correct" other members of the congregation or to contradict a pastor's message in public. Although these pastoral concerns are valid, the resultant effect may be the quenching of manifestations of the Spirit. Careful teaching and admonition from the pastor should be able to guide or restrain potentially disorderly expressions. The possibility for problems will always be present and some pastors will choose simply not to encourage prophecy rather than face the issue of dealing with disruptive phenomena.[19] A number of pastors have claimed that as their churches have grown, it has become logistically impossible to accommodate or guide prophecies from the congregational members. Prophecies can take up too much time and there is the danger of immature prophets or unknown visitors speaking forth. Often it is difficult for individual vocal expressions to be heard in larger auditoriums. Many larger urban churches now limit prophecies to the trained platform worship teams assisted by electronic amplification.

Other Pentecostal practices like corporate singing in the Spirit, praying in the Spirit, altar services for the baptism in the Holy Spirit, prayer for healing and calls for salvation, appear to have a more secure position in AoG ritual. Testimonies (of miracles, divine healing and personal salvation) appear to be less emphasized and may need attention. These oral and narrative expressions could be revitalized through the use of multimedia and prerecorded testimonies on DVD played in the service. As church services develop in response to the sophistication of growing churches, practices that were once encouraged to be spontaneous may need to be nurtured in a more organized manner.

Pentecostal pastors often claim there is no official order or "liturgy" of service, but a definite form has evolved. It varies from one church to another but the components are similar: a "praise and worship" segment, welcoming visitors, receiving tithes and offerings, a special musical item,

---

19. Ibid., 189–95.

announcements, preaching the word and an altar call. More traditional services last about two hours and the more contemporary to one-and-a-half hours. Openness to and mode of expression of Pentecostal manifestations vary. Some AoG pastors encourage such manifestations, others do not, and most seek a "middle of the road" experience. Older-style Pentecostal services attempt to ritualize classical Pentecostal experiences but increasingly pastors appear to be resisting approaches perceived to be inauthentic or culturally inappropriate. Some still use old forms to liven up formal Pentecostal ritual such as orderly hand clapping and responses such as "amen" and "halleleujah." Although these are often authentic, they at times can be routine as any set liturgy. Larger churches have professionalized their services, sometimes filmed for video production. Presentations are more professional, with a team of pastors and quality musicians who often seek to get audience response in a preplanned way. The operation of the gifts of the Spirit occurs mainly among those leading the meeting on the platform. Occasionally, the order of service is set aside as the power of the Holy Spirit takes over a service and the congregation collectively responds.

Spiritual/religious expressions that counter the planned ritual may leave a pastor-leader in an invidious position to work out what to do next and how to handle any problems that develop. It appears more pastors prefer routine to the potential dangers of experiences that could turn institutional order into chaos. Data from both the survey results and the key ministers' reflections suggest pastors are becoming less comfortable with individually expressed classical Pentecostal practices and are more likely to prefer the safety of institutional form or the combined worship experience to an experiential flare-up. To minimize potential inauthentic practices or disorder, pastors are increasingly dissuading individualized experiences in services and are emphasizing set programs, professionally run services and discouraging "emotionalism." Some churches may have controlled the spontaneous moving of the Holy Spirit to promote more institutional church growth. If the priesthood of believers in ministry and the impulse of spiritual gifts are to be continually revitalized, much influence is in the hands of the local pastor.

Dilemma of Power

The *dilemma of power* is about accommodation and acculturation. New converts demonstrate less interest in and loyalty to the organization than those who grew up in it. When denominations try to control their freedom by attempting to dictate solutions to tensions, it may produce a reaction resulting in the departure for newer, less organized and more charismatic churches. Another manifestation of this dilemma is the unprecedented involvement in politics by denominational leaders.[20] In Australia, the AoG is far more cautious in being identified with those of its favorite sons who have moved into the political arenas. Despite this, the AoG seems to be moving from the position of political passivity of its early founders.

This dilemma has been allowed to remain alive, allowing the accommodation process to proceed unnoticed. Poloma believes this process will continue unless a core value is endangered. For Pentecostals this core value "is a worldview in which religious [spiritual] *experiences* are central," not narrow doctrinal definitions of identity.[21] At the National Conference on 3 May 2005, President Brian Houston declared the AoG is never to be a political organization, yet pastors should encourage individual constituents called to enter politics in whatever party. Nevertheless, the new Family First Party does have close links to the AoG, with many of its members attending AoG churches.[22]

Dangers of Delimitation

The pastor's role most clearly embodies the tension between charisma and institutionalization as he or she struggles to avoid *delimitation*. This dilemma addresses the threat to following the leading of the Spirit, which tends to relativize the original religious message in relation to new conditions. In the AG in the United States, there has been successful pastoral resistance on issues most affecting their congregations (against legalism about divorce and remarrying being the best example) but often the letter of the law seeks to replace the spirit of charisma. In Australia sufficient influence from the AoG constituency resulted in the AoG's policy on divorce and remarriage being reviewed by the National Executive (adopted at National Conference, 2007). Poloma claims that in the North American experience, "pragmatism and expediency rather than prayer and dialogue are often the preferred methods for stilling controversy." She claims there has been a centralized

20. Ibid., 210.
21. Ibid., 161.
22. Cettolin, unpublished notes.

shift of power toward the AG's General and Executive Presbyteries at the expense of local churches.²³

The crucial issue for the AoG is whether pastors in its autonomous churches are able to retain the control of their centralized denominational government structure or whether the central structure will dominate its constituents. In Australia, the shift of power has been more personal; to those pastors adopting leadership-driven models of church government (as opposed to congregational models) and who have also secured Executive denominational positions. A point of departure from the AG model in North America is that in Australia most AoG State and National Executive members are unsalaried and continue to hold their own church pastoral positions and local power base with its local interests to protect. It may be that this locally empowered executive will find it is more able to represent local interests and resist growing central bureaucratic control.

Keeping the Dilemmas Viable

These dilemmas cannot be resolved without either quenching the Spirit of God and the manifestations of spiritual gifts or alternatively capitulating to disorder. To the extent that such tensions exist, charisma is alive and the Spirit of God has a freer reign within a healthy organization. Pentecostal spiritual experiences may be institutionally dangerous, but to silence them would be to remove the distinctive identity of Pentecostalism. The emphasis on autonomous local church self-government and "apostolic" leadership at executive levels within the AoG system seems to be promoting diversity of ministries and churches. AoG churches can attract very different types of socio-economic and racial groups and like-minded people from the larger neo-Pentecostal movement and the church at large. As a result, a wide variety from traditional to contemporary worship styles, are accommodated within the AoG. On the other hand it may be argued that as the larger mega-churches continue to flourish, the culture of the movement may be influenced away from diversity.²⁴

Importantly, Poloma's study shows that experiences of paranormal phenomena, including signs and wonders, divine healing and prophetic abilities are the best predictor of activities that would facilitate church growth. The indicators of some dilemmas reflect the burden institutionalization has

23. Poloma, *Assemblies of God at the Crossroads*, 162, 165–67, 210–11.
24. See Clifton, "Apostolic Revolution."

placed on charisma, whereas others reflect a healthy tension that allows charisma freedom to operate. Charisma is a factor in the rise and revitalization of movements but all too often it seems to depart quickly once it has completed the task of "institution-building." It may be even more fragile now, as modern institutions prefer efficiency and pragmatism than an elusive charisma.[25]

Biblical Analysis

Is such institutionalization of churches inevitable, according to scriptural precedent? Some scholars argue that a development can even be seen in the churches in the New Testament. A contrast has been emphasized between the Spirit-endowed ministries, seen in the Corinthian church, for example, with the concern for hierarchy and order evident in the Pastorals and the organization that emerged early in the second century. This is often seen as a response to a crisis stirred by a declining enthusiasm and expectation of an imminent parousia. However, the emphasis on official ministers over a non-ministering laity is far from the situation in the Pauline *homologoumena* (Rom, 1 & 2 Cor, Gal, Phil, 1 Thess, and Phlm) where all believers are seen as charismatics. The later development can be considered as "early catholic," an abandoning of the freedom of ministering by the Spirit for the safety of routinization of ministerial office and cultic celebration.[26]

Seeing the apostolic age in two distinct and contrasting church orders—"the charismatic" and "the institutional"—was given classic expression by Rudolf Sohm at the turn of the last century and it still attracts support.[27] The argument is that in the early Pauline epistles, the churches are free of structures and subject solely to the direction of the Holy Spirit in contrast to churches in Acts, the epistles of James, 1 Peter, 1 and 2 Timothy and Titus, where elders and institutional order are mentioned. This view sees two opposing pictures of the church with no middle ground.[28]

The weakness of this approach is that it is based on an idealistic, dichotomous understanding of social structures that may not correspond to actual historical reality. Weber made "the charismatic" and "the institutional" two ideal types against which phenomena could be measured and

---

25. Poloma, *Assemblies of God at the Crossroads*, 123, 232–36.
26. Harding, *What Are They Saying*, 14–15, 60–61.
27. See Dunn, *Jesus and the Spirit*, 199–258.
28. Giles, *Patterns of Ministry*, 9–12.

reality approximated more to one or the other. Scholars like Sohm confuse the notional with the actual. Some of the uncertainty comes from that fact that Weber took the term "Charisma" from Paul (via Sohm). Although both uses sometimes merge they must not be confused. Paul's understanding is theological, reflecting the way the Spirit of God works in individuals to empower them for ministry. Weber, on the other hand, seeks to provide a "value free" construct where charisma is applied to a certain quality of a person's personality by which he is considered extraordinary and endowed with supernatural, superhuman or exceptional powers or qualities.[29]

Is there some indication in the New Testament that Paul thought movement away from the freedom of the Spirit and spontaneity to more ordered church life is a detrimental development? The evidence suggests that it is not so straightforward. Paul takes distinct approaches with different churches. He advocates more order for the Corinthian church but allows for the freedom of the Spirit in the Pastorals while still watching out for heresies. Although church order at Corinth was charismatic, it also had institutional forms and while the church order in the Pastorals was more institutional, it also had charismatic elements; it was basic and not like the established structures in later centuries.[30] However, Weber's ideal type is still a useful framework to understand this development.

If we only have a short period of time for the New Testament and the second generation had not yet taken over, one would not expect a great deal of institutionalization. Some scholars see the New Testament covering a longer period and think the process to be so advanced they doubt if certain epistles were written by Paul. Arguments for authenticity are complex and beyond the scope of this book. There is no convincing reason to reject their authenticity and much seems to commend their early dates.[31]

We need to be cautious as most of the evidence is implied and not explicitly stated. Diversity can be over-emphasized and a linear framework of institutionalization imposed on Scripture rather than allowing it to speak for itself. Tidball believes "the brakes were not let off the process until after the end of the New Testament period" when the growth of offices and bureaucracy, stereotyping of worship, legalization of ethics, and the intellectualizing of Christianity became widespread. Later Montanism,

---

29. Ibid., 175–77.
30. Ibid., 9–10.
31. Tidball, *Introduction to the Sociology of the New Testament*, 128–29.

as a prophetic movement, emerged in the second century in reaction to these trends.[32]

Those who see a distinction between charismatic and institutional church order in the New Testament interpret Paul's understanding of ministry in the congregation to only be a matter of supernatural and episodic manifestation. This is an inadequate interpretation of Paul's understanding of "spiritual gifts" as he emphasizes every ministry is a gift from God. His term to interpret the various ministries in the life of a congregation is *charisma* (singular) *and charismata* (plural). In 1 Corinthians 12–14, Paul debates an elitist group that sees episodic manifestations of the Spirit as the mark of the spiritual person. He insists the Spirit has been given to all, not just leaders. The church is like a body in which every member makes a contribution (1 Cor 12:13–26) and this is to be understood as a *charisma* (1 Cor 12:4, 9). Tongues-speaking is a charisma, as is helping, administration, teaching, exhortation, leading, generosity and charitable acts (Rom 12:7, 28).[33]

Applying a sociological perspective to the New Testament, Tidball argues that by the time Paul had established his churches the pure charisma of Jesus had already been institutionalized in Jerusalem and routinized in Paul. "The Church then, in sociological terms was largely in its early days a charismatic group of the second generation."[34] Giles also argues that the process of institutionalization of the church begins early in the group around Jesus, although not consistently. Persecution and heresy may have encouraged it and an outbreak of charismatic gifts discouraged it. Paul's death would have hastened it, as the churches would have had to take full responsibility for their own life. Although this could be seen simply as a sociological phenomenon, it need not exclude other layers of explanation, including the Holy Spirit drawing the early Christians into stable and structured communities. Not all "institutionalization" is inevitably a work of human self-reliance against the freedom of the Spirit. Some structure and form could equally be the result of the innovative work of the Holy Spirit. The household setting of the early churches works against the view that the believers in the Pauline churches gathered in an unstructured free association where a fundamental social equality existed without any offices. It also fails to recognize that the emergence of office is just one part of

---

32. Ibid., 133–34.
33. Giles, *Patterns of Ministry*, 15–16.
34. Tidball, *Social Context of the New Testament*, 57.

institutionalization and it does not appreciate that in Paul's view the church "charisma" and office belong together.[35]

Margaret MacDonald argues that the world of the early Pauline believers was in fact a catalyst for change in the churches.[36] She locates the start of institutionalization with Paul himself who supports the various local offices arising naturally in the churches he addresses and values their independence. An increasing institutionalization in the Pauline corpus, testifies to the need to stabilize community life due to severe challenges by false teachers and criticism of the community's behavior from those outside. Leaders in the Pastorals are seen to be respectable male house-holders who conform to the ethical criteria affirmed by the Greco-Roman urban elites, and have the teaching aptitude required for church leadership. Only by maintaining these values and order could the church, as the "household" of God, hope to embrace the empire.[37]

Innovation and Routinization

Holmberg examines the New Testament evidence and interprets it through the lens of modern theoretical sociology, especially Weber's sociology of authority. He sees opposing forces interacting in a constant process of interplay evidencing the complexity in the early church. He concludes that a charismatic authority was "continuously being institutionalized and reinstitutionalized" through the interactions of persons, institutions and social forces within the church.[38] However, this picture is too unqualified to reality. It has been common to play off "charisma" and "office" against one another as representing opposite and irreconcilable poles, one of which was swallowed up and destroyed by the other in the course of early church history.

"Charisma" is seen as free, unstructured, prophetic leadership, deriving its authority from the inspiration of the Spirit, and responds in an ad hoc manner as needed. "Office" is seen as permanent, stable leadership by designated individuals based on legally constituted authority transmitted in a hierarchical succession. Stereotypically, charisma means freedom and spontaneity; office means stability, continuity and the eventual suppression

---

35. Giles, *Patterns of Ministry*, 10–15.
36. MacDonald, *Pauline Churches*, 9, 26.
37. Harding, *What Are They Saying*, 61–62.
38. Holmberg, *Paul and Power*, 198–201.

of charisma under the weight of its authority. This interpretation is simplistic. If "office" is already present in Paul's churches, it is equally true that "charisma" does not disappear in the later, more institutional church of the second and third centuries.

Osiek argues some hierarchical figures of that period, such as Ignatius of Antioch and Cyprian of Carthage, consider themselves "charismatics" possessing the spirit of prophecy and live according to its inspiration. Although there is a development of institutionalization in the early church, it cannot be blamed for the demise of charisma. The explanation is far more complex.[39]

An alternative interpretation of the development to institution is suggested. Rather than speaking of the "routinization of charisma," the process can be understood as the transformation of charismatic leadership and structure into other types. This is especially so if the charismatic authority is not a victim of institutionalization, but rather the initiator, as Holmberg finds Paul to be. When charisma seeks institutional manifestation for the sake of stability, order, and continuity, a new phase in the life of the movement is occurring which is neither better nor worse, but necessary for survival. The effect is more social control, less freedom from the pressure and ambiguity of living in an unstructured world, allowing further capacity for self-governed action. The apostolic church could then be described as an institutionalized charismatic movement begun through the inspiration of a dynamic leader who commanded authority and whose claim to revelation was compelling. Holmberg says this is a movement that followed the inevitable laws of nature by evolving structures and more permanent types of authority, which responded to the ongoing need for order. In the process, "the charism is not lost, but transformed into different shapes and manifestations."[40] Although Holmberg's critiques of Weber are an important contribution, not all will agree with his exegetical conclusions. Some see Paul as an advocate of unstructured freedom against later Christian institutionalism. Nevertheless, Holmberg strongly makes the case from textual data and sociological theory for the transition to institutional structure to be earlier than many thought.[41]

Holmberg criticizes Weber for underrating the complexity and for not considering the charismatic leader's role in the process as the main

---

39. Osiek, *What Are They Saying*, 77–78.
40. Holmberg, *Paul and Power*, 198–201.
41. Osiek, *What Are They Saying*, 78–80.

routinizing agent who wants to build a lasting community. "Dilemmas of institutionalization should not be confused with its driving forces." It is better to speak of the *institutionalization of charisma*. "Institutionalization is the term denoting the whole process, and is present from the very inception of the charismatic movement whereas routinization is only part of the process."[42] MacDonald agrees that Holmberg's corrections help to harmonize Weber's insights with the understanding of institutionalization as a process beginning in the early stages with institution-building impulses inherent in the charisma itself. It helps us understand how development in the early church proceeded and how the innovation is given permanence as a social structure.[43]

These insights help us to interpret the current developments in the AoG. Although it could be argued that the AoG pastors' (Pentecostal) spirituality is becoming more institutionalized, this does not mean it is necessarily more routinized or detrimental to the life and growth of the church. The existence of the dilemmas of institutionalization within the AoG referred to previously, point toward a healthy tension in the movement. It seems charisma has been allowed to operate and even "institutionalize" for the benefit of the growth of the AoG as the cultural context it finds itself in begins to change. Charisma is a factor in the rise and revitalization of the movement. It does not seem to have quickly departed once the construction of the denomination was completed but rather it has changed in its form and structure.

Theological Reflections

There is a widespread view in Protestant circles, especially Pentecostal/Charismatic ones, that the Spirit of God and church institutions are in contradiction (2 Cor 3:17). This view fails to understand the nature of church structures and the way the Spirit of God works. The result says Miroslav Volf, would be "pneumatic anarchy" as the only appropriate structure for the Pentecostal church.[44] We must go beyond a simplistic dichotomy of charisma versus institution, order versus freedom or Spirit versus structure. Pentecostal movements like the AoG are developing increasingly complex structures but also continuing to grow and flourish. The issue is not so

---

42. Holmberg, *Paul and Power*, 162–65, 176–78.
43. MacDonald, *Pauline Churches*, 14.
44. Volf, *After Our Likeness*, 234.

much whether growing institutionalization *in itself* is good or bad, but whether it is having detrimental effects on the Pentecostal spirituality of AoG pastors and churches. Clifton notes that institutions are central to human communities without which we have rampant individualism. Rather than overriding the original charisma, "it may be possible for institutional developments to encourage and enhance the charismatic orientation of the church."[45] The current changes in Pentecostal spirituality that this research has shown may indicate AoG pastors are "intuitively" responding to this need for "charismatic order" in their churches.

As Miroslav Volf points out, institutions are stable structures of social interaction. Every social unit as a group is already an institution. "Concrete sociality and institutionality are inseparable." You can only become a Christian and then live as one, through institutionalized procedures—confessing Jesus Christ as Lord, baptism, communion with the triune God and with each other. "The essential sociality of salvation implies the institutionality of the church. . . . The question is not *whether* the church is an institution but rather what *kind* of institution it is."[46]

In my view, Pentecostals, like those in the AoG, are living out a model of church that holds out a promise of transforming Christianity. However, this is occurring without much theological reflection, particularly in relation to the doctrine of the church. As we have seen in chapter one, this is an important issue as many Australians are saying spirituality is of vital interest to them, but not the institutional church. The influence of individualism means people will say that Christianity is not about church but a relationship with God. The church, however, is more than just an optional extra to faith and its institutional nature is an integral aspect of its constitution. It is necessary therefore to look at what Pentecostal ecclesiology may have to say to us about the nature of the church, including its institutional character. Hopefully this will provide some guidance for the future direction of Pentecostal movements like the AoG in their own social context.

Pentecostal Ecclesiology

According to Evangelical theologian Clark Pinnock, what Pentecostalism has to say about ecclesiology is more than academic:

---

45. Clifton, "Holy Spirit," 4.
46. Volf, *After Our Likeness*, 234–35.

> The gargantuan challenge that we face in mission is not something that can be effectively responded to on an individual basis.... The fact is that we are not meant to be isolated disciples but communities incorporated into the Spirit-filled body of Christ. Even our experiences with God are corporate, shared experiences, sustained by community. We cannot and are not meant to go it alone.[47]

Pinnock proposes a distinctly Pentecostal ecclesiology of power where the main aspect is believers endued with power to serve as anointed witnesses to the kingdom of God. Pentecostals experience God as empowering and commissioning for mission. The presence of the Spirit is a sign and foretaste of God's reign, which is even now breaking into the world. The church is the community of faith central to God's plan, called to witness to the character of his reign and to reveal the nature of his kingdom. God expresses himself to the world in the present through the church, by signs and wonders. This ecclesiology provides a unique way of interpreting the gospel as not only justification, forgiveness and a rational message, but also as a word of power that heals and delivers people in the here and now.[48] This model is a helpful starting point.

Veli-Matti Kärkkäinen provides further insights in relation to understanding the structure of the church from a Pentecostal perspective. He reports that in his involvement in the *Roman Catholic Church-Pentecostal Dialogue (1972–1989)*, one of the main issues of ecclesiology discussed was the relationship between the Spirit/charisma and institution. Whereas the Catholic Church has emphasized hierarchy, ordained ministry, church authority and sacraments, Pentecostalism as a recent revival movement, has generally emphasized the working of the charismata in the church. Pentecostals "were ready to go beyond the all-too-simplified dichotomy of 'charisma *versus* institution' to a more fruitful notion of church which is *both* Charismatic *and* has structure." For Pentecostals there is no one aspect to identify the "true nature" of a church as they see that the New Testament does not show us *the* structure but several types.[49]

The dialogue team sought to develop a Pentecostal view of the church as Charismatic fellowship: "*fellowship was a common experience of baptism into the body of Christ through the Spirit* (cf. 1 Cor 12:13)." This is a shared experience in the life of the community through the presence of the Spirit

---

47. Pinnock, "Church in the Power of the Holy Spirit," 149–50.
48. Ibid., 150–53.
49. Kärkkäinen, *Introduction to Ecclesiology*, 73–74.

and concretely lived out through the charismata, which is provided to *every* member. However, this emphasis on the charismatically constituted church does not mean stressing the charismata at the expense of structure and institutions which would be both sociologically and historically naïve.[50]

Trinitarian Ecclesiology

In seeking to understand Pentecostalism and charter a way forward recent scholarship on the Trinity is instructive. Initiated by Karl Barth's (1936) pioneering and imaginative work on this crucial doctrine, there has been a great renewal of interest in the Trinity. Theologians generally are agreed this doctrine is foundational to the Christian faith. They have also seen the practical and ethical implications of a doctrine of the Trinity that stresses mutuality, community and equality.[51]

A Trinitarian model of the church first of all gives place to all three persons in the Trinity—the Father, Son and Spirit. It also emphasizes co-equality and community. All three persons are fully omnipotent: indivisible in power and authority. They are bound together and united in self-giving love and "perichoresis" (interpenetrating communion). All work inseparably and they are never divided. In every work of God all three persons work as one, but each makes a distinctive contribution. The Father creates and as creator gives form and structure to all life, which is his gift. This includes human institutions as part of his creation. The Son redeems those who believe in him. The Spirit is the one who sanctifies and empowers. "Thus, all the divine works, whether creation, redemption, sanctification, or any other, while in each case more particularly the work of one member than the others, are nonetheless the work of the entire Trinity."[52]

Believing that God's life should inform their own life, Christians have long recognized that there is an analogical relationship between Trinitarian relations and human life. This is needless to say limited because God in eternity represents perfection and we humans are part of a fallen world. As a result, in our world among other things, provisional hierarchies are needed to order communal life. Volf says, "The human dimension of ecclesial institutions requires that the assignment of certain roles (charismata)

---

50. Ibid., 74–75.
51. Giles, *Trinity and Subordinationism*, 86–87, 103–5
52. Erickson, *Making Sense of the Trinity*, 67.

must always be viewed as provisional."[53] Thus, the doctrine of analogy requires that we move from God to humanity not vice versa.[54] It also arguably suggests a non-hierarchical model for human relationships. Each person of the Trinity is differentiated from the others, "yet of equal value and dignity and each responds to the others in self-giving love, working together in perfect harmony."[55]

As this doctrine is a natural starting point for theological reflection it enriches and informs the doctrines of the church and ministry in a number of ways. First, the doctrine of the Trinity reminds us that in some distinct ways each member of the Trinity: Father, Son and Spirit, contributes to the life of the church. This insight is a corrective to theologies, which all too often focused almost exclusively on one of the three persons of the Trinity. Liberal traditions emphasize God the Father, who is seen as the Father and creator of all; the Catholic and Reformation traditions which have almost exclusively focused on Christ, (the former, in the sacraments and the latter through the preached Word); and third, the Pentecostal/Charismatic movement which at times can so focus on the Spirit that the Father and Son get eclipsed. A truly Trinitarian theology of the church follows Paul who taught that all of ministry flows from the contribution of all three, Father, Son and Spirit (1 Cor 12:4–6; cf. 2 Cor 13:13; Eph 4:3–6). It also sees the church as called into existence by the Father, redeemed by the Son and empowered by the Spirit (Eph 1:3–14).

In relation to the issues discussed in this Research Project, a Trinitarian perspective is very helpful. Theologians have long held that ordered life is a gift of God the creator. Thus they speak of government (Rom 13:1–50) and marriage (Gen 2:23–25), as "created orders." On this basis we should think of church government and church structures, what we have called "institution," as a gift of God the creator. He is the one who gives stability to all social institutions, including the church. It is however, Christ who brings "the new creation" (2 Cor 5:17). He is the one who redeems those living in the fallen creation. He restores what sin has distorted. He brings into existence a community where God the creator is understood as Father. In this community the Spirit is the divine transforming presence. He makes fallen creatures redeemed by Christ new people, binding them together in

---

53. Volf, *After Our Likeness*, 244.

54. Giles, unpublished notes.

55. Giles, "Holy Trilemma," 7–8.

community—a community that is a foretaste of the perfect community to be known in heaven.[56]

Another way the contemporary renewal of the doctrine of the Trinity has enriched ecclesiology is by seeing the Trinity as an image, an *eikon* or model of ecclesial life. This is a common theme in contemporary theological work but Miroslav Volf has possibly most carefully and productively explored this matter. He is quite clear that the movement must be from God to the church and human relations, not vice-versa. He is highly critical of the circular reasoning of scholars who begin with their doctrine of the church and then develop their doctrine of God, arguing that their doctrine of the Trinity supports their ecclesiology. For Volf, the Trinity is a community of three "co-equal" divine persons where none is before or after (Athanasian Creed) bound together in self-giving, united together in being and action, mutually indwelling one another in perichoretic (interpenetrating) community.[57] In this Trinitarian view, if humanity is relational and if God is social, then the church might be seen as mirroring the Trinity, suggesting a Trinitarian ecclesiology. God who is a communion of love, exercises power that is interactive and shared but not dominating, and calls out a community to share his glory (John 17:24–26). It suggests we can envision the church as the image of the Trinity, following its relational and dynamic pattern.[58]

Many theologians argue that the doctrine of the Trinity should practically inform all human relationships and therefore challenges all forms of human domination and becomes a charter for liberation.[59] According to Pinnock, when we confess that God is triune we are affirming that the eternal life of God is personal life in relationship, that God exists in community and that the life of God is in essence self-giving love. The church therefore should seek to be a temporal mirror of these Trinitarian relations:

> We are the community that is called to be, on the finite level, the kind of reality that God is in eternity. The divine dance (perichoresis) supplies the basis for personal dynamics of the community. The church needs to order its life in this manner so as to echo the community of Father, Son and Spirit.[60]

56. Giles, unpublished notes.
57. Volf, *After Our Likeness*, 191–200; 234–35.
58. Pinnock, "Church in the Power of the Holy Spirit, 153–54.
59. Giles, "Holy Trilemma," 7–8.
60. Pinnock, "Church in the Power of the Holy Spirit," 154.

If the Trinity is meant to be a model for us to follow in relating to each other, then the implications are that we should be concerned to function in a relationship of equality and mutual respect. We would need to understand that although people have different gifting they are as important to God as we are, and we must treat them as equals. If the Holy Spirit indwells all Christians, then the judgment and insight of each should be equally valued. Although this does not indicate the sort of church government we should have, it does mean that it is improper to dominate or coerce people. Some will have different responsibilities and play more significant parts in church life or in decision making, due to their gifting, experience or spiritual maturity. Just as in a sporting team there will be functional differences but all are, and should be seen as significant, and treated with respect (James 2:1–7; 1 Cor 12:22–27).[61] This has implications for Pentecostal pastors in taking individual member's contributions seriously but also for church members to allow those gifted to lead to be able to do without being resisted or disrespected (Heb 13:17).

A Community of the Spirit

Pinnock suggests the church is to be an anointed witness to the kingdom of God and therefore it must be a community of the Spirit. The Pentecostal model of church as a fellowship of the Spirit is an expression of the free-church model, but as we have seen with Pentecostal spirituality, there is an experiential approach that emphasizes an encounter with the supernatural. As with many Pentecostal churches, in the AoG we now see a new model of church emerging, where people gather not to hear a sermon as in the Reformed tradition or to witness a sacerdotal liturgy as in the Catholic tradition, but to experience the presence of the living God where the meeting pulsates with life. The power of the original Pentecost event is continued in ritual, God is expected to move with power, and there is broad participation by an empowered laity. The location of the church in this model is where the Spirit is present in power and its prominent "mark" is the manifestations of the presence of God (which we have sought here to measure, to some extent, in AoG pastors and churches). The key and defining thing is to have a living experience of the Spirit. This does not exclude the Word and sacraments but the fellowship must transcend the merely institutional.[62]

61. Erickson, *Making Sense of the Trinity*, 84–96.
62. Pinnock, "Church in the Power of the Holy Spirit," 156–57.

Such a church will need a continuing charismatic structure where there is a gifted community. The New Testament makes no distinction between charismatic and non-charismatic believers. The one Spirit baptizes all into the body of Christ and, all experience the Spirit. However, that does not mean there is no place for offices. There is a need for certain institutional aspects of church that are part of the continuing charismatic structure. As discussed previously, in any social movement an institutional dimension is needed in order for it to function and continue. What is essential from a biblical perspective is that the institutional elements be functional, flexible, effective and appropriate to facilitate the work of God. Pinnock reminds us that the Spirit is fundamental for the church and must be given primacy over structures and offices, even though they too are Spirit-given.[63] It is essential that the charismatic leadership offices and charismatic pastoral offices facilitate the Spirit's work, including through charismatic lay people. Somehow this must be given primacy over contemporary structures, programs and developments.

Popular author and pastor Bill Johnson of Bethel Church, Redding, California, says that after the Reformation the pulpit became the center of the church worship service rather than the experience of the Presence of God. "Israel camped around the Presence of God" in the tabernacle, "while the church often camps around a sermon." He says that somehow the church must "adjust whatever is necessary to rediscover the practical nature of the Presence of God being central to all we do and are."[64]

Trinitarian Pentecostalism

As Trinitarian Pentecostals, the AoG's understanding of the work of the Spirit cannot be divorced from the Spirit's relationship to the Father and the Son. The doctrine of the Trinity should inform church life and assist us in our theological reflections on both the doctrines of the church and of Spirit baptism. Simon Chan says that to reflect upon the Spirit's work in the Trinity is to discover the point of integration between belief and practice in the affection, as brought out by Land.[65] Following Augustine's thinking, the Spirit is the bond of love between the Father and Son and between Christ and the church. Pentecostal spirituality, which looks at the Trinity from the

---

63. Pinnock, "Church in the Power of the Holy Spirit," 161–62.
64. Johnson, *Hosting the Presence*, 169–70.
65. Land, *Pentecostal Spirituality*.

perspective of the Spirit, could be characterized by a special configuration of religious affections (orthopathy), which enlivens right belief (orthodoxy) and issues in right practice (orthopraxy). Theologically speaking, one could say "Pentecostal spirituality is essentially affective trinitarianism."[66]

Volf agrees that we need to think of the church as the image of the triune God following the relational and dynamic pattern of the Trinity.[67] He suggests a participatory ecclesiology where the presence of Christ in the Spirit, which constitutes the church, is mediated not simply or primarily through the ordained ministers but the whole congregation. He argues that we should carefully listen not only to tradition, but to the emerging voices of thriving growing churches, both in the West and especially outside in the Majority world.[68] The AoG is one of the many of these new Pentecostal church voices that can speak to us about developing a contextualized ecclesiology. He sees God's eschatological new creation as the all-embracing framework for an appropriate understanding to help identify and locate the church: Wherever the Spirit of Christ, which as the eschatological gift anticipates God's new creation in history (see Rom 8:23; 2 Cor 1:22; Eph 1:14), is present in its *ecclesially constitutive* activity, there is the church. The Spirit unites the gathered congregation with the triune God and integrates it into a history extending from Christ, indeed, from the Old Testament saints, to the eschatological new creation.[69]

Volf believes the church reflects in a broken way the eschatological communion of the entire people of God with the triune God in God's new creation, and so its institutions should correspond to the Trinity as well. That they are able to do this comes from the charismata that structure the church. Relations between charismatics are to be modeled after triune relations. The institutionality of the church can be conceived in correspondence to the Trinity only because the Trinity itself is in a certain sense an "institution." One cannot imagine the Trinity without a stable structure of social interaction between the divine persons. Of course the Trinity is an institution only analogously and cannot only be considered "from above" but also from the church's created and historical nature. A purely sociological basis neglects the fundamental core of the church as a communion with the triune God. On the other hand, an exclusively Trinitarian base fails to

---

66. Chan, *Pentecostal Theology*, 29, 32–33.
67. Volf, *After Our Likeness*, 214–20.
68. Ibid., 11–13.
69. Ibid., 129.

do justice to the character of the church as a community in history on a journey toward its eschatological goal.[70]

Volf's model takes symmetrical relations within the Trinity as a premise. As a result the more a church is characterized by symmetrical and decentralized distribution of power and freely affirmed interaction, the more it will correspond to the Trinity's communion. Relations between the charismata would be reciprocal and symmetrical; all members of the church have charismata and all are to engage their charismata for the good of all the others. The concrete forms of reflecting the Trinity in the church are shaped not only by the model of the Trinity but also by the various cultural contexts in which the church finds itself. The ministries of the church must be understood pneumatically, including the offices. Volf sees the offices like the charismata, as institutions, but are distinguished from them according to the kind and degree of institutionalization.[71]

In Pentecostal churches like the AoG, the universal baptism in the Spirit is meant to make it possible for every member of the assembly to give messages in tongues, provide interpretations and speak prophetically. Even the administration of the sacraments (baptism and the communion), is not limited to the ordained pastor. At its best, the office of pastor is meant to encourage these experiences and so enhance rather than contradict the priesthood and prophethood of believers.[72]

The participative model of the church requires more than just values and practices that correspond to participative institutions. Volf says it needs the vivifying presence of the Spirit without which it becomes just as sterile as a hierarchical church and will have to operate without the participation of most of its members or with more subtle and open forms of coercion. Where does this leave Pentecostal churches like the AoG if the conclusions of this study are correct, in that there is significant decline in the participation of the ordinary member in the public gifts? Volf's insight seems pertinent: "Successful church life must be sustained by deep spirituality."[73] In the light of this it is argued that reviewing Spirit baptism may help to ensure that the life of the presence of the Spirit remains constant.

---

70. Ibid., 235.
71. Ibid., 239–57.
72. Clifton, "Holy Spirit and the Leadership Structures," 6.
73. Volf, *After Our Likeness*, 257.

Reflections

Theology of Spirit Baptism

Perhaps the changes discovered in Pentecostal spirituality point toward the deduction that now is the time to look at a reworking of the doctrine of Spirit baptism. Although Western classical Pentecostals usually define themselves in terms of the doctrine of "initial evidence," from the evidence presented in this study AoG pastors seemed to be more concerned with the wider experience of the working of the Holy Spirit and the practice of spiritual gifts. Their emphasis is falling on experiential spirituality rather than formal theology, doctrine of the Holy Spirit or of Spirit baptism.

As discussed previously, the theological link between tongues-speaking and Spirit baptism was first formulated as the doctrine of "consequence" or "initial evidence" at the turn of the twentieth century and continues to be a fundamental doctrine of most classical Pentecostal denominations, including the AoG. The doctrine of "subsequence" had earlier origins in the Holiness movement, which interpreted Wesley's teachings to identify a "second work of grace" subsequent to conversion. "Finished Work" Pentecostals came to identify this as the baptism in the Spirit, although holiness Pentecostals added Spirit baptism to the two works of grace and spoke of it as a "third work of grace." Classical Pentecostals claim the normative pattern of Spirit baptism is the "initial evidence" of speaking in tongues. Classical Pentecostals usually support the doctrines of "consequence" and "subsequence" by referring to the book of Acts (2:4; 8:4–19; 10:44–48; 19:1–7) and 1 Corinthians 14:5, 18 as "normative models for all Christians." They explain Paul's implied statement that not all speak in tongues (1 Cor 12:30) by distinguishing between tongues as a "sign" (as evidence of Spirit baptism) and tongues as a "gift" (not for all believers to use in church meetings).

Most Pentecostals believe Spirit baptism is a distinct and separate experience that follows salvation with the result that some Christians can "be saved," but not yet filled with the Spirit.[74] There has been contentious debate over the doctrines of "consequence" and "subsequence." In 1970 James D. G. Dunn[75] argued that Spirit baptism is synonymous with conversion and charged Pentecostals as attempting to separate one single divine act into two works of God. In the nineties, Pentecostal scholars, Menzies, Synan and

---

74. Anderson, *Introduction to Pentecostalism*, 190–92.
75. Dunn, *Baptism in the Holy Spirit*.

Spirit Freedom and Power

Stronstad[76] countered that Dunn is reading Pauline theology into Lukan accounts. They agreed that Paul's theology of the Spirit primarily emphasized the role of the Spirit in conversion but that Luke's theology is mainly charismatic and prophetic, emphasizing empowering for mission. Pinnock believes the "second blessing" doctrine was a reaction to bad teaching and practice in the church.[77] John V. Taylor said, "It is better to call it incorrectly a second blessing and lay hold of the reality of new life in Christ than to let the soundness of our doctrine rob us of its substance."[78]

A number of classical Pentecostal pioneers (even Seymour) eventually challenged the assumptions of "initial evidence." In recent years Gordon Fee, a New Testament scholar and AG minister, suggested that Pentecostals could describe speaking in tongues as a valid "repeatable" experience but not claim it was "normative," as the doctrine of "subsequence" is not clearly taught in the New Testament. In response, Pentecostal scholars, particularly Menzies and Synan,[79] have defended "evidential tongues," mainly based on Luke's unique pneumatology. About the same time, the AG in the North America reaffirmed their belief in classical Pentecostal pneumatology in the General Council in 1991.[80]

As can be seen, there are a number of contrary views on Spirit baptism and tongues, even within the Pentecostal/Charismatic movement. Some Pentecostals and Charismatics, while agreeing there is a distinct experience of Spirit baptism, think that tongues *may* follow this distinct experience but are not essential evidence of the baptism. Others see it as an initiatory experience that is part of the conversion process and the gifts of the Spirit are given to all believers. Still others, especially Catholic Charismatics, see Spirit baptism in sacramental terms, as a release of the Spirit already given in baptism (but not so distinctive). In the attempt to formulate a theology of the Spirit, Pentecostals have been criticized as having fallen as much as Catholics and Protestants for the temptation to systematize the movement of God's free Spirit. The debate about Dunn's approach (conversion/initiation) is not just about where the baptism in the Spirit fits into the order

---

76. Menzies, "Luke and the Spirit"; Synan, "Role of Tongues"; Stronstad, *Scripture and Theology*.

77. Pinnock, "Church in the Power of the Holy Spirit," 167–69.

78. Taylor, *Go-Between God*, 202.

79. Menzies, "Luke and the Spirit"; Synan, "Role of Tongues."

80. Anderson, *Introduction to Pentecostalism*, 192–95.

of experience, but whether it is distinctive and discernible.[81] Menzies and Shelton both attempt to support the classical Pentecostal view that Luke-Acts is about a baptism in the Spirit as power for service to be experienced after conversion.[82] Aspects of this were also held by some earlier charismatic approaches. However, the recent release, renewal or "Third Wave" approaches weaken the concept of a distinctive experience.

Because of the different positions on the central point of classical Pentecostal theology, Anderson argues it needs to be evaluated from a different perspective and suggests that Steven Land's approach on "Pentecostal spirituality" offers a way out of impasse.[83] Land says Pentecostalism cannot be identified with a rationalistic evangelicalism and that the starting point for Pentecostal theology must be its distinctive spirituality: the Holy Spirit who is "God with us"[84] For most Pentecostals and Charismatics, the experience of the immanence of God in the fullness of the Spirit through prayer, worship and the gifts of the Spirit is still a main characteristic and is at the heart of their theology, especially if it does not need to be harmonized with conservative Evangelical theology. Land shows the relationship between spirituality and Pentecostal theology and defines the essential spirituality of Pentecostalism as "the integration of beliefs and practices in the affections which are themselves evoked and expressed by those beliefs and practices." He argues Pentecostalism emphasizes the Holy Spirit as a starting point for a distinctive approach to theology as spirituality. To "do theology is not to make experience the norm, but it is to recognize the epistemological priority of the Holy Spirit in prayerful receptivity."[85]

Integration—Trinitarian Spirit Baptism

Pentecostal scholar Frank D. Macchia, develops a corrective on the Trinity referred to above by recent theologians to so much earlier theologizing by Pentecostals. He offers a plausible systematic approach that seeks to integrate Pentecostal perspectives with Evangelical theology. With regard to Pentecostal ecclesiology, Macchia believes that baptism of the Spirit can be the organizing principle. He says this is responsive to different accents

---

81. Massey, "Response to Rethinking Spirit Baptism," 174.
82. Menzies, "Luke and the Spirit"; Shelton, "Reply to James D. G. Dunn."
83. Land, *Pentecostal Spirituality*.
84. Anderson, *Introduction to Pentecostalism*, 195–96.
85. Land, *Pentecostal Spirituality*, 38–39.

of Pentecostalism as a global movement and also broader ecumenical discussion. Accents such as regeneration, sanctification, Spirit filling, coming kingdom of God in power, missions, and charismatic giftings (including prophecy, tongues, and healing) "can be drawn to create a vision of the church as the central and unique sign of grace in an increasingly graceless world."[86] He agrees that Luke's Spirit baptism doctrine is charismatic and to do with empowerment of the church as a witness, while Paul's is primarily soteriological, to do with being in Christ. He explains that Stonstrad's position sought to avoid reading the Pauline meaning into Luke.[87] He further argues the theology of Spirit baptism, which Menzies and Menzies[88] hold as a charismatic experience distinct from Christian initiation, was based only on Luke. Although Macchia essentially agrees with both these authors, he wants to integrate Paul and Luke's understandings of Spirit baptism and include other canonical voices. He suggests we should speak of a [Trinitarian] theology of Spirit baptism that is both soteriologically *and* charismatically defined, an event with more than one dimension because it is eschatological in nature and not wholly defined by Christian initiation. He finds help in the popular charismatic distinction between Spirit baptism *theologically* defined as a divine act of redemption and initiation into the life of the kingdom involving faith and baptismal sealing, and Spirit baptism as empowerment for Christian life and service that involves *experience(s)* of Spirit baptism and filling in life. However, this distinction still lacks a broader framework to integrate these dimensions. As concepts of the church involve us in competing notions of initiation and of the church in general, Macchia suggests a broader eschatological interpretative framework for Spirit baptism as a Trinitarian act. Hopefully this will provide fresh insights and new common ground and thereby help "mend the rift" between Spirit baptism as a soteriological and as a charismatic category.[89] It is also of interest that Volf finds a similar eschatological frame of reference for his Trinitarian conception of the church. However as seen from this research Pentecostal movements like the AoG, are lessening their emphasis on Spirit baptism. It is also being displaced as the main theological distinctive (the "crown jewel") among some Pentecostal theologians. Macchia gives four reasons for this: early fragmentation of initiation from charismatic empowerment

---

86. Macchia, *Baptized in the Spirit*, 256.
87. Stronstad, *Scripture and Theology*.
88 Menzies and Menzies, *Spirit and Power*.
89. Macchia, *Baptized in the Spirit*, 15–17.

occasioned by the shift historically from sanctification to Spirit baptism; the challenge of diversity in the early history and the global expanse of Pentecostal beliefs; the shift of doctrinal focus from Spirit baptism to eschatology among Pentecostal theologians and; the shift under Hollenweger as to what is most distinctive to Pentecostal theology, from doctrinal to theological method—oral, narrative or dramatic theology.[90]

Macchia cautions against this and seeks to answer what many who follow Stronstad's and Menzies' exegetical conclusions have not asked; what might a systematic (and I would add truly Trinitarian) doctrine of Spirit baptism look like in the light of Paul and the rest of the New Testament? He argues the Spirit baptismal metaphor can be descriptive of both God's action in inaugurating the kingdom of God and our empowered witness to it. He achieves this by using a broader pneumatological framework, implied by Luke but explicitly provided by Matthew, Paul and John. Macchia believes this task is urgent, "since a compartmentalization of the Pentecostal understanding of Spirit baptism as a post-conversion charismatic empowerment will fail to enrich our understanding of the soteriological functions of the Spirit and vice versa."[91]

Part of the reason early Pentecostals resisted a formal connection between sanctification and Spirit baptism was the connection forged early on between Spirit baptism and speaking in tongues. In Macchia's view this separation occurred only because they defined sanctification narrowly and negatively as a cleansing from sin, whereas sanctification is also positively a consecration unto God in preparation for a holy task. He concludes that Spirit baptism as an experience of charismatic power and enrichment cannot be separated from regeneration/sanctification and Christian initiation.[92] Although I am not convinced that this was only reason for the separation of Spirit baptism and sanctification, a wider category of Spirit baptism would I believe help Pentecostals see the Trinitarian involvement of God in salvation in more biblical terms:

> The Trinitarian structure of Spirit baptism thus has a two-way movement: from the Father through the Son in the Spirit, and then from the Spirit through the Son toward the Father. We thus

---

90. Ibid., 19–60.
91. Ibid., 59.
92. Ibid., 83–84.

pray and relate from God, in God and to God (Rom 11:36). Spirit baptism involves all three.[93]

In Macchia's schema of the eschatological significance of Spirit baptism in ushering in the kingdom of God, he sees it important to develop the elements of life in the Spirit, justification, sanctification, and charismatic empowerment, in a fully Trinitarian context. He notes that Hendrikus Berkhof wisely isolated all three as elements of baptism in the Spirit and faulted the history of pneumatology in the West for focusing exclusively on justification and sanctification to the neglect of Pentecostal focus on the vocational or charismatic dimension of life in the Spirit.[94] Macchia says Spirit baptism as an eschatological participation in the kingdom of God by faith involves Christian initiation *and* a release of the Spirit in life for power in witness:

> That Pentecostals ask the church to seek a definite experience of Spirit baptism as a renewal of faith and a prophetic anointing for service with or distinct in time from Christian initiation need not be interpreted as taking anything away from Christian initiation as that decisively initial point of identification with Christ as the one in whom all spiritual blessings may be found (Eph 1:3). Rather, the experience of Spirit baptism cherished by Pentecostals brings to our awareness theological insights inherent in the meaning of the initiation itself.[95]

It is suggested that this broader and truly Trinitarian framework to understand Spirit baptism not only more accurately reflects the changes and current practices in the AoG's Pentecostal spirituality, but also continues the process of Pentecostal spirituality informing on Pentecostal theology. It could be integrated with Volf's eschatological conception of the church. It avoids an outdated Pentecostal exclusivity and narrow focus on evidential tongues. It would also inform and enrich our understanding of the soteriological functions of the Spirit (as well as empowerment) and provide a basis to foster better inter-church understanding and relations.

---

93. Ibid., 117.
94. Ibid., 128–29.
95. Ibid., 153.

7

Conclusion

Change Is in the Air

THE STUDY I CONDUCTED of the lead pastors' spirituality in my own Pentecostal movement has elicited lessons that are instructive for Pentecostal, Charismatic, Evangelical and other renewal movements, particularly in the Western world. A convergence of evidence indicates that Pentecostal spirituality is changing for many pastors and may well be a phenomenon found in other similar movements and denominations.

It seems fairly clear that in recent years at the beginning of the twenty-first century there is developing less emphasis on the classic expressions of Pentecostal experience. Pastoral leaders are more frequently using mainline (non-Pentecostal) forms in their private devotional practices and there is a clear decrease in classical Pentecostal practices in church services. At the same time however, their churches are becoming more involved in community engagement and service. While there is a move away from classical Pentecostal beliefs and attitudes, increasingly more "Charismatic" and "Third Wave" beliefs and traditional mainline approaches are being adopted.

Although the pastors' Pentecostal spirituality is becoming more "institutionalized," this does not mean it is necessarily more "routinized" or is necessarily detrimental to the life and growth of their church. The existence of the "dilemmas of institutionalization" indicates the existence of a healthy tension. The charismata have been allowed to operate and even "institutionalize" for the benefit of the growth of the movement as the cultural context it finds itself in begins to change. As is often seen through history, charisma is a factor in the rise and revitalisation of a movement. In this case it has not quickly departed once the construction of the movement was completed, rather it has changed in its form and structure.

The influence of the "Charismatic" renewal and "Third Wave" movements has revitalised a classical Pentecostal denomination, illustrating a sociological principle operating through Pentecostalism. As Allan Anderson says, "constant change is here to stay." This movement of churches is an example of a new Pentecostalism emerging, and it is "unlikely that this process of renewal, institutionalization and further change will slow down."[1]

The development of charismatic leadership into a more institutional type, where spontaneity and freedom gives way to order and organisational structure is probably inevitable if any social group is to going to continue to survive. The problem arises when an overly negative value judgment is made about this type of development. This view would see a pristine Christianity that only existed for a brief period, of maybe one generation—that of Jesus and Paul. Once the influence of routinization and institutionalization kicks in, the original impetus is diluted into something of lesser value in the later New Testament and subsequent years, interspersed by periodic renewal movements, which eventually suffer the same fate. This is an overly simplistic and dismal view of the history of the Christian church.[2]

Without question the Spirit of God is continually involved in periods of renewal to reverse any petrifying effects of institutionalisation in the church. Equally however, why could not the Spirit of God also be behind some of the processes creating new structures and institutional systems seeking to preserve this very new life in the Spirit that has come in embryonic form? Deliberate and Spirit-inspired developments in the institutionalisation of charisma, is very different from the fossilisation that occurs in its "routinization." The New Testament itself gives evidence of some such development in the church organisation to preserve stability, order and survival.

Our Australian case study seems to point to the conclusion that Pentecostal movements are reaching more people resulting in the development of organisational structures needed to oversee the growing movements. An essential aspect of Pentecostal spirituality is its flexible, adaptive and innovative nature operating in a specific social and cultural context. The Spirit of God is creatively inspiring the development of new structures and forms to reach

---

1. Anderson, *Introduction to Pentecostalism*, 164–65.
2. Osiek, *What Are They Saying*, 78.

Conclusion

and disciple more people. The development of Pentecostal spirituality into its current forms as shown by the leaders' practices, evidences the influence of institutionalization. This has actually facilitated the growth and preservation of the movement. Pentecostalism with its flexibility in the Spirit has an "innate ability to make itself at home in almost any context."[3] Pentecostals are exercising their freedom in the Spirit to develop their own culturally relevant "contextualised" expressions of spiritual life, church and ministry.

From a sociological perspective, it can be argued that the charisma in this movement is institutionalizing for its own survival. From a theological perspective however, it is my view that the Spirit of God is creating new structures to nurture the growth of this new life. It is only when this structure begins to fossilize and the function and purpose for which it was originally intended, is forgotten, that problems and difficulties emerge. In that situation rather than the structure serving the Spirit of God and charisma, it becomes an end in itself. It is not only human beings but also their man-made structures that suffer from the effects of the fall. Church history is full of repeatedly alternating patterns of petrification, institutionalization and revitalization. Sometimes this occurs within the structures themselves, sometimes people have been forced out of the church or movement causing yet another new institution to be born. Tidball laments, "Our world today is littered with dead structures that no one has had the courage to bury."[4]

The negative aspects of institutionalization can only be overcome by going back to basics. A movement's goals must be constantly reviewed and reached. Whether the best people and most suitable people are leading needs to be continually reviewed. Movements need to be alert to the perils of mixed motives, unwieldy bureaucracy, the lowering of standards and the fossilisation of principles. They need to be vigilant to any new people God may wish to lead the movement in a continual process of renewal. Above all, people in the movement need to be continually pointed toward the source of all life and vitality, the Spirit of God himself.

Christian Schwarz in *Natural Church Development* has put forward the thesis that healthy growing churches are those able to maintain a reciprocal relationship; a creative tension between the static pole of institutionalism and the dynamic pole of charisma, between organism and organization, between the freedom of the Spirit and human structures. There is "bipolarity" evident in the New Testament where the church is referred to with both

---

3. Anderson, *Introduction to Pentecostalism*, 283.
4. Tidball, *Introduction to the Sociology of the New Testament*, 135–36.

static and dynamic images. Typical dynamic images describe the church as a "body" (Rom 12:4–8). Static images are taken from the world of architecture and construction (1 Cor 3:10). Some scriptures actually combine the dynamic and static images together, such as "living stones" (1 Pet 2:5; Eph 2:21; 4:12; 1 Cor 3:9).[5]

The continuing success and ongoing viability of churches as part of renewal movements will depend on whether they are able to maintain this tension between institutionalization and the freedom of the Spirit. An innovative flexible relationship needs to be preserved between the experience of the Spirit and the charismatic authority of local lead pastors on the one hand, and denominational structures with bureaucratic authority on the other.

The recent emphasis on contemporary relevance and leadership by many Pentecostal and other evangelical church movements is often the expression of a desire to be outward looking, a corrective of attitudes of inwardness and of an excessively internal spirituality, that of a "bless me club." It is based on a desire to be obedient to the scriptural purpose of reaching people outside the church. However, there is always a danger in the compromise that accommodation brings. As a result the tension between organism and organisation needs to be continually monitored. In my view the key is in the hands of Spirit-empowered local church pastors and their own practices of spirituality in both private and public church settings.

Spiritual Freedom and Flexible Structures

If it is true, that our age suffers from an, "ecstasy deficit," as Harvey Cox argues, then the restoration of the operation of the spiritual gifts will enable people to become more aware of deeper insights and feelings.[6] If these "spiritual" experiences are merely for personal gratification, then the emphasis on the experience of the gifts of the Spirit is detrimental to a healthy, holistic Christian life. If they do enhance a sense of belonging to community, meet felt needs, and bring a greater love for God and one's neighbor, then the emphasis on the Spirit is to be embraced.[7]

The research data from the study and the reflections of key ministers provides insights into current Pentecostal practices of the pastors and their

---

5. Schwarz, *Natural Church Development*, 84–99.
6. Cox, *Fire from Heaven*, 83, 86.
7. Anderson, *Introduction to Pentecostalism*, 283–84.

Conclusion

churches in a Western setting. They are an indication of where Pentecostalism is heading and the future impacts on the freedom of the Spirit and the structure of the church. The work of the Spirit needs to extend beyond individualistic spiritual practices and private experiences of the gifts of the Spirit toward more combined, corporate and unified expressions.

It is not difficult to conclude that the growing Pentecostal movement in urban Western settings will continue to develop more professional and charismatically structured church organizations. Some ministers and leaders view the move toward contemporary cultural relevance as involving a more integrated and holistic spirituality than the traditional or classical early Pentecostal expressions. At times, the classical Pentecostal practices could be self-serving and inward, rather than reflecting a Spirit-empowered Christianity that has a focus on reaching unchurched people. However, there are a significant number of ministers who are concerned that contemporary approaches will lead to a dilution of certain key elements of Pentecostal spirituality. It would be of some concern to many in the movement that the survey *Index* measuring frequency of Pentecostal experiences and practices, together with other data, does indicate a tendency toward decline in the practices of Pentecostal spirituality in the pastors. This may have adverse implications for the future direction of Pentecostal phenomena in church services.

A certain level of conflict or tension must be tolerated if the experience of the immanent presence of the Spirit and the practice of the spiritual gifts is to continue its role in the movement's Pentecostal spirituality. Sociologically speaking, the institutional dilemmas cannot be silenced without also extinguishing "charisma" or adversely affecting the institution. They help not only in institution-building but also in creating an environment that is receptive to charisma. Conflict is lethal to a group only when it attacks a "core value," but over peripheral issues it may actually help in advancing social structures.

The Pentecostal movements all have their share of strong personalities with differing views over doctrine and ministry practice. The key issue is whether the structure is flexible enough to allow diversity without fracturing its unity. Entry of those from the wider Charismatic movement and those pursuing contemporary, relevant and/or modern approaches to ministry dilute the classical expressions of Pentecostal spirituality. However, it inevitably also increases attendance and brings openness to the experience of the immanent presence of the Spirit. It brings a healthy distrust of routine ritualism or reliance on early Pentecostalism's enshrined doctrinal statements and institutionalism. Rather than being a threat, these tensions are signs of new life and strength.

With many pastors studying contemporary methods, skills, practices, models of leadership and church growth, there is an increasing emphasis on institutional factors for success. Many successful Pentecostal ministers, speakers and authors, usually attribute their institutional growth and success to prayer, revelation and the power of the Holy Spirit. Nevertheless, this message is often easily lost as others seek to imitate their programs and methods. It is often forgotten that these have come out of these successful ministers own personal relationship and experiences with the Spirit of God. The paradox of power is a core value that requires a continued balance between programs and spiritual power—between natural efforts and supernatural assistance.[8]

To ensure the survival of the freedom of the Spirit and the practice of the gifts a tolerance for ambiguity is called for. Margaret Poloma goes so far as to claim that to silence the dilemmas of institutionalization would be the end of the uniqueness of Pentecostal spirituality:

> Weeds as well as the wheat will grow within the institutional matrix. . . . Ambiguities and tensions are sure to accompany the presence of charisma, but leaders would do well to heed the admonition of Jesus, who when asked if the weeds should be pulled replied: "No, because while you are pulling the weeds you may root up the wheat with them. Let them both grow together until the harvest (Matthew 13:29–30)."[9]

The future for Pentecostal movements holds the promise of greater institutional growth and development along with attempts to maintain the freedom of the Spirit. At the same time there is with Pentecostal movements like ACC a growing alignment with successful growth oriented contemporary styled churches and networks. These churches and groups embrace numerical growth and contemporary relevance but deny the validity of some aspects of Pentecostal spirituality, particularly with experiences of the Spirit and practice of the spiritual gifts. This may have implications for the direction of Pentecostal spirituality within the institutional setting of these Pentecostal movements. The weeds and the wheat may need to be allowed

---

8. Poloma, *Assemblies of God at the Crossroads*, 237–38.
9. Ibid., 240–41.

Conclusion

to grow together until the Lord of the harvest determines time is up for these movements.

A Call for Action

There is a need for the continuing development of a contextualised and mature spirituality among Pentecostal pastoral leaders that improves the effectiveness of church life and mission. A major challenge for these leaders is how to allow the Holy Spirit freedom to move and for charisma to flourish. Leaders must continually seek the release of a truly people-led movement empowered by the Spirit along with a genuine and authentic practice of the gifts of the Spirit. The local church pastor needs to facilitate the work of the Spirit through all the members. This is the key person to guide and correct the operation of the gifts in the public church services, modelling and encouraging this in fresh and culturally relevant expressions. Although elders and other lay church leaders have a role to play and may be delegated various tasks and roles, in the typical Pentecostal church the pastor exercises the key leadership responsibility in teaching and nurturing lay people's development and operation of the gifts of the Spirit.

Recovering the spontaneous and oral aspect of early classical Pentecostal spirituality without sacrificing intellectual rigour and reflection must be encouraged. Emphasising ongoing experiences and encounters with the immanent presence of God at and after conversion in Spirit baptism needs to be fostered and a less rigid doctrinaire approach to the identity of who Pentecostals are, needs to be encouraged. A reworking of the traditional theological boundaries of Spirit baptism will assist pastors and churches not to neglect a powerful spiritual metaphor for both Christian initiation and ongoing post-conversion charismatic empowerment.

The "priesthood of believers" in ministry and the momentum of the spiritual gifts need to be continually revitalised, and it is mainly in the hands of the local church pastor. If the typical public weekend church service is no longer an appropriate venue for the operation and the regulation of these spiritual gifts, then another needs to be made, whether a mid-week meeting, a prayer meeting, a specialised training event or in small groups meetings. The approach and style should be relevant and sensitive to the specific cultural context. A specified time and space within the corporate service for "body ministry" should be made. Pastors need to give direction, teach and lead people in how to minister to each other by exercising the gifts of the Spirit for healing, prophecy, words of wisdom and so forth. Workshops and seminars on the operation of the gifts of the Spirit in a balanced, contemporary and pastorally guided approach need to be reinstated. Unless this is seriously attended to, the stimulus of the charisma may be marginalised or significantly diminished.

Pastors as leaders in a Pentecostal/Charismatic movement need to be open and honest about spiritual experiences and enthusiasm without glossing over any inauthentic practices. Emotional expressions should be genuine and reflective of contextual cultural forms rather than importing cultural expressions from "old time Pentecostal services" or incompatible social expressions and cultural contexts. A continued quest for psychological, intellectual and spiritual integration must be valued and sought after, without downplaying any individual aspect. There needs to be a recovery of the early eschatological and apocalyptic fervour without becoming overly "otherworldly." The goal should be to produce a greater openness to interracial fellowship and leadership and also to see more female participation in ministry and leadership. A recovery of the value of being "not of this world" within increasingly affluent Western cultural contexts will require church leadership to provide great examples of sacrificial and generous giving to counter the influence of materialism and consumerism.

The continuation of a missional outward-looking Pentecostal spirituality should be encouraged. The focus should remain on reaching the non-churched with the gospel of Jesus Christ as well as pursuing social transformation and providing pastoral care to those in need. Social righteousness and justice must not be ignored in bringing people to personal salvation and righteousness. In the past, Pentecostals could have been accused of practising a spirituality that has little concern for social transformation and preaching a gospel that either spiritualises or individualises social problems and advocacy for the oppressed has generally not found a voice in its spirituality. Initiatives to help the poor are increasing and must be encouraged to continue. For Pentecostal spirituality to be identified with liberating social action, a discernment of the forces of deception will be needed. Being filled with the Spirit also includes an involvement in discernment of the truth to uncover the travesties that maintain injustice, oppression and lack of compassion toward the marginalised within global communities.

A reinforcement of biblical authority with a Spirit empowered approach to Scripture is needed but with a widening of the full counsel of the

Word of God. It must go beyond the narrow foci of personal development and success, to issues of character, holiness and discipleship. A re-emphasis on the reflective forms and practices of spirituality and not only the more activist practices should be seriously considered. As suggested a well-worked theological Trinitarian perspective of Spirit baptism as a divine act in both inaugurating the kingdom and eschatological participation in the kingdom is required.

The autonomy of local Pentecostal churches should be maintained while accepting the benefits of leadership in the denomination's executive positions. However, the organisational advantages of leadership-driven models of church structure must not be allowed to sideline ordinary lay people's maximum participation in prayer, witness, testimony and decision-making.

Reform and Renewal

For many contemporary Pentecostal movements like the AoG, the pastors' spirituality remains Pentecostal, but is delivered and styled in increasingly "contemporary clothes." It is still oriented on *experience* with the Holy Spirit but is reflecting a more educated and affluent Western cultural context. It demonstrates the importance of holding firm to principles and revealed truths, not forms and traditions. It does however, point to the conclusion that leaders must constantly go back to the painful self-critical task of bringing the structures and programs of their movement into line with its original stated aims.

The distinctive nature of Pentecostal spirituality is based on a desire to reform and renew the church. Pentecostal pastors expressing this emergent spirituality are grappling to relate to their specific Western cultural context. It is clear that change is taking place in their spirituality and it is with mixed ramifications for them as pastors and leaders and for their church organizations. However, not all institutional developments are the result of the negative forces of routinization and spiritual decline. Although social scientists generally claim that when a religious movement moves out of the "charismatic" phase and becomes institutionalized, its growth rate slows significantly, my research has shown that this is not inevitably so. Instead of being overcome by modernity and secularisation, the signs are that Pentecostal movements are able to grow and continue to adapt to social change.

Renewal and positive change are possible within church movements and denominations!

Nevertheless, it is vital that church movements continue in a process of a holistic personal renewal of its leaders and pastors. Ongoing corporate renewal together with healthy sustainable growth by the working of the Spirit of God is possible. Finally, a clear framework for future action is proposed that calls for an engagement in the theological development of a truly Trinitarian Pentecostal church structure and a renewed emphasis on teaching about Spirit baptism:

> Now there are different kinds of spiritual gifts, but it is the same Holy Spirit who is the source of them all. There are different kinds of service in the church, but it is the same Lord we are serving. There are different ways God works in our lives, but it is the same God who does the work through all of us. (1 Cor 12:4–6 NLT)

Bibliography

Adam, Peter. *Hearing God's Words: Exploring Biblical Spirituality.* Downers Grove: Apollos/InterVarsity, 2004.
Ainge, Keith. "AOG Exceeds 1,000 Churches in Australia." *Now! Assemblies of God in Australia*, winter 2003.
Albrecht, Daniel E. "Pentecostal Spirituality: Ecumenical Potential and Challenge." *Cyberjournal for Pentecostal-Charismatic Research* 2 (1997). http://www.pctii.org/cyberj/cyberj2/albrecht.html.
———. *Rites in the Spirit: A Ritual Approach to Pentecostal/Charismatic Spirituality.* Journal of Pentecostal Theology Supplement Series 17. Sheffield: Sheffield Academic, 1999.
Alcorn, Wayne. "ACC Overview". Letter 2015. Email.
Anderson, Allan. *An Introduction to Pentecostalism: Global Charismatic Christianity.* Cambridge: Cambridge University Press, 2004.
———. "World Pentecostalism at a Crossroads." Introduction to *Pentecostals after a Century: Global Perspectives on a Movement in Transition*, edited by edited by Allan H. Anderson and Walter J. Hollenweger. Journal of Pentecostal Theology Supplement Series 15. Sheffield: Sheffield Academic Press, 1999.
Archer, Kenneth J. *Pentecostal Hermeneutics: Retrospect and Prospect.* Journal of Pentecostal Theology Supplement Series 8. Sheffield: Sheffield Academic, 1996.
Assemblies of God in Australia. Assemblies of God in Australia website, 2004. http://wwwaogaustralia.com.au/default.asp?ContentID=1000802.
———. *Constitutional Documents (Including Assemblies of God Church World Missions Missionary Constitution).* Mitcham, Victoria, April 1993.
———. *Directory, National Office of the Assemblies of God in Australia.* Mitcham, Victoria, 1998.
———. *Ministers Bulletin.* Mitcham, Victoria, May 1984.
———. *Now!* Mitcham, Victoria, winter 2003.
———. *Our History 1937–1997: 60 Years of Assemblies of God in Australia.* Video recording. Mitcham, Victoria: Ambassador Television, 1997.
———. *Victoria/Tasmania, Minister's Manual.* June 15. Mitcham, Victoria: National Office of the Assemblies of God in Australia, 1994.

Bibliography

Aumann, Jordan. *Christian Spirituality in the Catholic Tradition*. San Francisco: Ignatius, 1985.
Australian Christian Churches. *ACC News*. November 2001. Baulkham Hills, NSW.
———. *ACC EMag*. Special edition 3, September 2015. http://www.acc.org.au/news-media/emag-issue-no-32015.
———. *Australian Evangel*. Official organ of the Assemblies of God. Mitcham, Victoria, 1928–present.
Ayuk, Ayuk Ausaji. "The Pentecostal Transformation of Nigerian Church Life." *Asian Journal of Pentecostal Studies* 5 (2002) 189–204.
Babbie, Earl. *The Practice of Social Research*. Belmont, CA: Wadsworth, 1998.
Bagnall, Diana. "Give Me That New Time Religion: Born Again Hip and Booming." *Bulletin*, April 11, 2000, 27–31.
Baker, Chris. "Next Generation Essay: Experiencing the Supernatural." *Australasian Pentecostal Studies* 9 (2006) n.p. http://aps-journal.com/aps/index.php/APS/article/view/89/86.
Barrett, David B. "Annual Statistical Table on Global Mission 1997." *International Bulletin of Missionary Research* 21 (1997) 24–25.
Barrett, David B., and Todd M. Johnson. "Annual Statistical Table on Global Mission 2002." *International Bulletin of Missionary Research* 26 (2002) 22–23.
———. "Status of Global Mission, 2002, in Context of Twentieth and Twenty-First Centuries." *World Evangelization Research Center: Pointing the Way to the Least Evangelized*. 2002. www.gemwerc.org/gd/findings.htm.
Barth, Karl. *Church Dogmatics*. Vol. 1.1. Translated by G. T. Thomson. Edinburgh: T. & T. Clark, 1936.
Baumgärtel, Friedrich. "Spirit in the OT." In *Theological Dictionary of the New Testament*, edited by G. Kittel and G. Friedrich, translated by G. W. Bromiley, 6:359–68. Grand Rapids: Eerdmans, 1968.
Bellamy, J., and Ruth Powell. "2001 Church Attendance Estimates National Church Life Survey." *Pointers* 14 (2004) 15.
Bellamy, J., et al. *Why People Don't Go to Church*. Adelaide: NCLS Research, 2002.
Berkhof, Hendrikus. *Doctrine of the Holy Spirit*. Richmond, VA: John Knox, 1964.
Berkhof, Louis. *Systematic Theology*. 4th ed. Grand Rapids: Eerdmans, 1949.
Bevans, Stephen. *Models of Contextual Theology*. Maryknoll: Orbis, 1992.
Beyer, Peter. *Religion and Globalisation*. London: Sage, 1994.
Blalock, Hubert M., Jr. *An Introduction to Social Research*. Englewood Cliffs, NJ: Prentice-Hall, 1970.
Blumhofer, Edith L. *Restoring the Faith: The Assemblies of God, Pentecostalism, and American Culture*. Urbana: University of Illinois Press, 1993.
Bonino, José Míguez. "Changing Paradigms: A Response." In *The Globalization of Pentecostalism: A Religion Made to Travel*, edited by Murray W. Dempster et al., 116–23. Oxford: Regnum, 1999.
Booth, Wayne C., et al. *The Craft of Research*. 2nd ed. Chicago: University of Chicago Press, 2003.
Bosch, David J. *Transforming Mission: Paradigm Shifts in Theology of Mission*. Maryknoll: Orbis, 1991.
Bruner, Frederick Dale. *A Theology of the Holy Spirit: The Pentecostal Experience and the New Testament Witness*. Grand Rapids: Eerdmans, 1970.

Bibliography

Burgess, Stanley M., et al., eds. *Dictionary of Pentecostal and Charismatic Movements (DCPCM)*. Grand Rapids: Zondervan, 1988.

Burgess, Stanley M., and Eduard M. Van Der Maas, eds. *The New International Dictionary of Pentecostal and Charismatic Movements*. Rev. ed. Grand Rapids: Zondervan, 2002.

Burns, Robert B. *Introduction to Research Methods*. 4th ed. Frenchs Forest, NSW: Langman, 2000.

Campbell, R. Alastair. *The Elders: Seniority within Earliest Christianity*. Edinburgh: T. & T. Clark, 1994.

Cargal, Timothy B. "Beyond the Fundamentalist-Modernist Controversy: Pentecostals and Hermeneutics in a Postmodern Age." *Pneuma* 15 (1993) 163–87.

Carmines, Edward G., and Richard A. Zeller. *Reliability and Validity Assessment: Series Quantitative Applications in Social Sciences*. London: Sage, 1979.

Carson, D. A. *The Gagging of God: Christianity Confronts Pluralism*. Leicester, UK: Apollos, 1996.

Cartledge, David. *The Apostolic Revolution: The Restoration of Apostolic and Prophetic Ministry in the Assemblies of God in Australia*. Chester Hill, NSW: Paraclete Institute, 2000.

———. *Chester Hill Miracles*. Sydney: Paraclete Ministries, 1997.

Cartledge, Mark J. "Practical Theology and Charismatic Spirituality: Dialetics in the Spirit." *Journal of Pentecostal Theology* 10 (2002) 93–109.

Cettolin, Angelo U. "AOG Pentecostal Spirituality in Australia: A Comparative Study of the Phenomenon of Historic Spirituality and its Contemporary Developments within the Assemblies of God in Australia." DMin diss., Australian College of Theology, 2006.

———. Unpublished notes of sessions at Assemblies of God in Australia National Conference, 2–6 May 2005.

Chan, Simon. *Pentecostal Theology and the Christian Spiritual Tradition*. Journal of Pentecostal Theology Supplement Series 21. Sheffield: Sheffield Academic, 2000.

Chant, Barry. Editorial. *Pentecostal Charismatic Bible Colleges Journal* (2002). http://pcbc.webjournals.org/articles/1/03/2002/3041.htm.

———. *Heart of Fire: The Story of Australian Pentecostalism*. Rev. ed. Unley Park, Australia: House of Tabor, 1984.

———. "The Spirit of Pentecost: Origins and Development of the Pentecostal Movement in Australia, 1870–1939." PhD diss., Macquarie University, Sydney, 1999.

Chapman, Graeme. "Theology, Spirituality and Ministry." *St. Mark's Review* 144 (1990) 22–27.

Clark, Matthew S. "Pentecostal Hermeneutics: The Challenge of Relating to (Post)-Modern Literary Theory." *Spirit and Church* 2 (2000) 67–93.

Clifton, Shane. "The Apostolic Revolution and the Ecclesiology of the AoGA." *Australasian Pentecostal Studies* 9 (2006) n.p. http://aps-journal.com/aps/index.php/APS/article/view/85/82.

———. "The Holy Spirit and the Leadership Structures of the Assemblies of God in Australia." *Pentecostal Charismatic Bible Colleges Journal* 1 (2006) 1–10. http://webjournals.ac.edu.au/ojs/index.php/PCBC/article/view/8863/8860.

Conn, Harvie M. *Eternal Word and Changing Worlds: Theology, Anthropology and Mission in Trialogue*. Grand Rapids: Academic, 1984.

Cox, Harvey. *Fire from Heaven: The Rise of Pentecostal Spirituality and the Shaping of Religion in the Twenty-First Century*. London: Cassell, 1996.

Bibliography

Cross, Terry L. "A Response to Clark Pinnock's 'Church in the Power of the Holy Spirit.'" *Journal of Pentecostal Theology* 14 (2006) 175–82.
Crouch, Donna. "The Leadership Pipeline: 8 Ways to Create a Leadership Pipeline for Women." *ACC EMag*, special edition 3, September 2015, 18–20.
Dayton, Donald. *The Theological Roots of Pentecostalism*. Grand Rapids: Zondervan, 1987.
Deere, Jack. *Surprised by the Voice of God*. Eastbourne, UK: Kingsway, 1996.
De Matviuk, Marcela A. Chavan. "Latin American Pentecostal Growth: Culture, Orality and the Power of Testimonies." *Asian Journal of Pentecostal Studies* 5 (2002) 205–22.
Dempster, Murray W., et al., eds. *The Globalisation of Pentecostalism: A Religion Made to Travel*. Oxford: Regnum, 1999.
Donovan, Vincent J. *Christianity Rediscovered: An Epistle from the Masai*. London: SCM, 1978.
Dunn, J. D. G. *Baptism in the Holy Spirit: A Re-examination of the New Testament Teaching on the Gift of the Spirit in Relation to Pentecostalism Today*. London: SCM, 1970.
———. *Jesus and the Spirit: A Study of the Religious and Charismatic Experience of Jesus and the First Christians as Reflected in the New Testament*. London: SCM, 1975.
———. *Unity and Diversity in the New Testament*. London: SCM, 1977.
Dupré, Louis, et al., eds. *Christian Spirituality: Post Reformation and Modern*. New York: SCM, 1989.
Dyrness, William A., ed. *Emerging Voices in Global Christian Theology*. Grand Rapids: Zondervan, 1994.
Edgar, Brian. "Spirituality: Sacred and Secular." *Working Together* 2 (2004) 14–15.
Elliott, John H. "Elders as Honored Household Heads and Not Holders of 'Office' in Earliest Christianity." *Biblical Theology Bulletin* 33 (2000) 1–8.
Erickson, Millard J. *God In Three Persons: A Contemporary Interpretation of the Trinity*. Grand Rapids: Baker, 1995.
———. *Making Sense of the Trinity: Three Crucial Questions*. Grand Rapids: Baker, 2000.
Fee, Gordon D. "Baptism in the Spirit: The Issue of Separability and Subsequence." *Pneuma: Journal of the Society for Pentecostal Studies* 7 (1985) 88–91.
———. *Gospel and Spirit: Issues in New Testament Hermeneutics*. Peabody, MA: Hendrickson, 1991.
———. *Listening to the Spirit in the Text*. Grand Rapids: Eerdmans, 2000.
———. *Paul, the Spirit, and the People of God*. Peabody, MA: Hendrickson, 1996.
Ferguson, Adele. "Prophet-Minded: Pentecostal Churches Are Not Waiting to Inherit the Earth; They Are Taking It Now, Tax-Free." *Business Review Weekly*, May 26–June 1, 2005, 34–41.
Ferguson, Sinclair B., et al., eds. *New Dictionary of Theology*. Leicester, UK: Inter-Varsity, 1988.
Foster, R. *Prayer: Finding the Heart's True Home*. London: Hodder & Stoughton, 1992.
Gallup. "Religion: Gallup Historical Trends." http://www.gallup.com/poll/1690/religion.aspx.
Gause, R. Hollis. "A Pentecostal Response to Pinnock's Proposal." *Journal of Pentecostal Theology* 14 (2006) 183–88.
Gibbs, Eddie. *Body-Building Exercises for the Local Church*. London: Falcon, 1979.
Giles, Kevin. "The Holy Trilemma." *Grid: A Christian Leadership Letter* 3 (2002) 7–8.
———. *Patterns of Ministry among the First Christians*. Blackburn, Victoria: Collins Dove, 1989.
———. "The Quest for Spirituality?" *Grid: A Christian Leadership Letter*, winter 1996.

Bibliography

———. *The Trinity and Subordinationism: The Doctrine of God and the Contemporary Gender Debate*. Downers Grove: InterVarsity, 2002.

———. Unpublished notes and transcripts of conversations, during April and June 2006. Melbourne, Australia, 2006.

Gilliland, Dean S., ed. *The Word among Us: Contextualizing Theology for Mission Today*. Dallas: Word, 1988.

Good News. Pentecostal Mission (later Apostolic Mission), Melbourne, 1910–1934.

Grant, Paul E. *What Does It Mean to Be a Pentecostal? Life and Ministry in the Holy Spirit*. Coopers Plains, Queensland: PacRim, 2005.

Grey, Jacqueline. "Prophetic (M)others: Judges 4–5, Pentecostalism, and the (De)construction of Women Ministers." *Australasian Pentecostal Studies* 7 (2003) 35–90.

Grossman, Cathy Lynn. "Poll: Americans Stretch the Truth on Attending Church." *Religion News Service*, May 17, 2014. http://www.religionnews.com/2014/05/17/christians-church-atheists-prri.

Grunlan, Stephen A., and Marvin K. Mayers. *Cultural Anthropology: A Christian Perspective*. 2nd ed. Grand Rapids: Zondervan, 1988.

Guenther, M. *Holy Listening: The Art of Spiritual Direction*. Boston: Cowley, 1992.

Guinness, O. *Fit Bodies Fat Minds: Why Evangelicals Don't Think and What to Do about It*. Grand Rapids: Baker, 1994.

Hadaway, C. Kirk, and Penny Long Marler. "How Many Americans Attend Worship Each Week? An Alternative Approach to Measurement." *Journal for the Scientific Study of Religion* 44 (2005) 307–22. http://onlinelibrary.wiley.com/doi/10.1111/j.1468-5906.2005.00288.x/abstract.

Hagberg, J. O., and R. A. Guelich. *The Critical Journey: Stages in the Life of Faith*. Salem, WI: Sheffield, 1995.

Harding, Mark. *What Are They Saying about the Pastoral Epistles?* New York: Paulist, 2001.

Harvest Bible College. *Harvest Bible College Student Handbook 2001*. Melbourne, 2001.

Hesselgrave, David J. *Communicating Christ Cross-Culturally*. 2nd ed. Grand Rapids: Zondervan, 1991.

Hesselgrave, David J., and Edward Rommen. *Contextualisation: Meanings, Methods, and Models*. Leicester, UK: Apollos, 1989.

Hiebert, Paul G. *Anthropological Insights for Missionaries*. Grand Rapids: Baker, 1985.

———. *Anthropological Reflections on Missiological Issues*. Grand Rapids: Baker, 1998.

———. "Conversion, Culture and Cognitive Categories." *Gospel in Context* 1 (1978) 5–9.

———. *Cultural Anthropology*. 2nd ed. Grand Rapids: Baker, 1983.

Hollenweger, Walter J. "The Black Roots of Pentecostalism." In *Pentecostals after a Century: Global Perspectives on a Movement in Transition*, edited by A. H. Anderson and W. J. Hollenweger, 33–44. Sheffield, UK: Sheffield Academic, 1999.

———. "The Contribution of Critical Exegesis to Pentecostal Hermeneutics." *The Spirit and Church* 2 (2000) 7–18.

———. "From Azusa Street to the Toronto Phenomenon: Historical Roots of the Pentecostal Movement." *Concilium* 3 (1996) 3–14.

———. *The Pentecostals*. London: SCM, 1972.

———. "Pentecostals and the Charismatic Movement." In *The Study of Spirituality*, edited by C. Jones et al., 549–54. London: SPCK, 1986.

Holmberg, Bengt. *Paul and Power: The Structure of Authority in the Primitive Church as Reflected in the Pauline Epistles*. Philadelphia: Fortress, 1978.

———. *Sociology and the New Testament: An Appraisal*. Minneapolis: Fortress, 1990.

Bibliography

Holt, Bradley P. *A Brief History of Christian Spirituality*. Oxford: Lion, 1993.
Horton, Stanley, ed. *Systematic Theology: A Pentecostal Perspective*. Springfield, MO: Logion, 1994.
Huggett, Joyce. "Understanding One Another." *Reality* 1 (1994) 15–20.
Hughes, Philip. *Australia's Religious Communities*. CD-ROM. 2nd ed. Christian Research Association, 2004.
―――. *The Pentecostals in Australia*. Canberra: Australian Government, 1996.
―――. "Religion in the 2001 Census." Christian Research Association. 2002. www.cra.org.au/pages/00000055.cgi.
―――. *Research Methods for Ministry and Ministry*. CD-ROM. Nunawading, Victoria: Christian Research Association, 2003. www.cra.org.au.
―――. "Spirituality as an Individual Project." Christian Research Association. 2001. www.cra.org.au/pages/00000071.cgi.
―――. "Working Globally, Thinking Locally." *Pointers* 13 (2003) 7–10.
Hughes, P., et al. *Believe It or Not: Australian Spirituality and the Churches in the 90s*. Kew, Victoria: Christian Research Association, 1995.
―――. *Religion: A View from the Australian Census*. Kew, Victoria: Christian Research Association, 1993.
―――. *Religion in Australia: Facts and Figures*. Kew, Victoria: Christian Research Association, 1997.
Hutchinson, Mark. "The New Thing God Is Doing: The Charismatic Renewal and Classical Pentecostalism." *Australasian Pentecostal Studies* 1 (1998) 5–21.
―――. "'The Normal Vision': Revival Thought in a Leading Australian Pentecostal Journal (Australian Evangel and Glad Tidings Messenger) 1928–1948." *Australasian Pentecostal Studies* 8 (2003) 1–16. http://aps.webjournals.org/articles/1/07/2004.
Hutchinson, Mark, and Edmund Campion, eds. *Long Patient Struggle: Studies in the Role of Women in Australian Christianity*. Sydney, NSW: Centre for the Study of Australian Christianity, 1994.
Inglehart, Ronald, and Wayne E. Baker. "Modernization, Cultural Change, and the Persistence of Traditional Values." *American Sociological Review* 65 (2000) 19–51.
Isaac, Stephen, and William B. Michael. *Handbook in Research and Evaluation: A Collection of Principles, Methods, and Strategies Useful in the Planning, Design, and Evaluation of Studies in Education and Behavioral Sciences*. San Diego: Educational and Industrial Testing Services, 1997.
Jagelman, Ian. "Church Growth: Its Promise and Problems for Australian Pentecostalism." *Australasian Pentecostal Studies* 1 (1998) 27–40.
Johns, Jackie David. "Pentecostalism and the Postmodern Worldview." *Journal of Pentecostal Theology* 7 (1995) 73–96.
―――. "Yielding to the Spirit: The Dynamics of a Pentecostal Model of Praxis." In *The Globalization of Pentecostalism: A Religion Made to Travel*, edited by Murray W. Dempster et al., 70–84. Carlisle, UK: Regnum, 1999.
Johnson, Ben C. *Pastoral Spirituality*. Philadelphia: Westminster, 1988.
Johnson, Ben C., and A. Dreitcer. *Beyond the Ordinary: Spirituality for Church Leaders*. Grand Rapids: Eerdmans, 2001.
Johnson, Bill. *Hosting the Presence: Unveiling Heaven's Agenda*. Shippensburg, PA: Destiny Image, 2012.
Johnson, Philip. "Do-It-Yourself Spirituality: Effectively Engaging Today's Seekers." *Working Together* 2 (2002) 1–4.

Bibliography

Jones, Cheslyn, et al., eds. *The Study of Spirituality*. London: SPCK, 1986.
Kaldor, Peter, et al. "Spirituality and Wellbeing in Australia." NCLS Occasional Paper 6. November 2004. Part of the Wellbeing and Security Study, a joint project of ANGLICARE Sydney and NCLS Research, Edith Cowan University, and Deakin University.
Kärkkäinen, Veli-Matti. *An Introduction to Ecclesiology: Ecumenical, Historical and Global Perspectives*. Downers Grove: InterVarsity, 2002.
———. *Pneumatology: The Holy Spirit in Ecumenical, International, and Contextual Perspective*. Grand Rapids: Baker, 2002.
Kay, William K., and Anne E. Dyer, eds. *Pentecostal and Charismatic Studies: A Reader*. London: SCM, 2004.
Kerr, Natalie. "Report on Women Holding Credentials in the Assemblies of God in Australia." Assemblies of God website, 2002. http://wwwaogaustralia.com.au/default.asp?ContentID=1000802.
———. "Revised Report on the 2002 Church Census Figures." Assemblies of God website, 2004. http://wwwaogaustralia.com.au/default.asp?ContentID= 1000802.
Kirk, Jerome, and Marc L. Miller. *Reliability and Validity in Qualitative Research Methods*. Vol. 1. London: Sage, 1986.
Klein, William W., et al. *Introduction to Biblical Interpretation*. Dallas: Word, 1993.
Kleinknecht, Hermann. "Pneuma in the Greek World." In *Theological Dictionary of the New Testament*, edited by Gerhard Kittel, and Gerhard Freidrich, 334–59. Grand Rapids: Eerdmans, 1968.
Kraft, Charles H. *Anthroplogy for Christian Witness*. Maryknoll: Orbis, 1998.
———. *Christianity in Culture: A Study in Dynamic Biblical Theologizing in Cross-Cultural Perspective*. Maryknoll: Orbis, 1979.
Labovitz, Sandford, and Robert Hagedorn. *Introduction to Social Research*. New York: McGraw-Hill, 1971.
Lancaster, Sarah Jane, ed. *Good News*. Monthly publication of the Good News Hall, North Melbourne, 1910–1936.
Land, Steven J. "Pentecostal Spirituality: Living in the Spirit." In *Christian Spirituality: Post Reformation and Modern*, edited by L. Dupré et al., 479–99. New York: SCM, 1989.
———. *Pentecostal Spirituality: A Passion for the Kingdom*. Journal of Pentecostal Theology Supplement Series 1. Sheffield: Sheffield Academic, 1993.
Leech, K. *Soul Friend: A Study of Spirituality*. London: Sheldon, 1977.
Leedy, Paul D. *Practical Research: Planning and Design*. 6th ed. Upper Saddle River, NJ: Merrill, Prentice-Hall, 1997.
Lickert, R. *A Technique for the Measurement of Attitudes*. New York: McGraw-Hill, 1932.
Lingenfelter, Sherwood G. *Agents of Transformation: A Guide for Effective Cross-Cultural Ministry*. Grand Rapids: Baker, 1996.
Luzbetak, Louis J. *The Church and Cultures: New Perspectives in Missiological Anthropology*. Maryknoll: Orbis, 1996.
Ma, Wonsuk. "Biblical Studies in the Pentecostal Tradition: Yesterday Today and Tomorrow." In *The Globalization of Pentecostalism: A Religion Made to Travel*, edited by Murray W. Dempster et al., 52–69. Carlisle, UK: Regnum, 1999.
Maas, R., and G. O'Donnell. *Spiritual Traditions for the Contemporary Church*. Nashville: Abingdon, 1990.
Macchia, Frank D. *Baptized in the Spirit: A Global Pentecostal Theology*. Grand Rapids: Zondervan, 2006.

Bibliography

———. "Pinnock's Pneumatology: A Pentecostal Appreciation." *Journal of Pentecostal Theology* 12 (2006) 167–73.

———. "The Question of Tongues as Initial Evidence: A Review of Initial Evidence." In *Pentecostal and Charismatic Studies: A Reader*, edited by Gary B. McGee, 110–12. London: SCM, 2004.

———. "The Struggle for Global Witness: Shifting Paradigms in Pentecostal Theology." In *The Globalization of Pentecostalism: A Religion Made to Travel*, edited by Murray W. Dempster et al., 8–29. Carlisle, UK: Regnum, 1999.

MacDonald, Margaret Y. *The Pauline Churches: A Socio-historical Study of Institutionalization in the Pauline and Duetro-Pauline Writings*. Cambridge: Cambridge University Press, 1988.

Mackay, Hugh. *Reinventing Australia: The Mind and Mood of Australia in the Nineties*. Pymble, NSW: Angus & Robertson, 1993.

———. *Turning Point: Australians Choosing Their Future*. Sydney: Macmillan, 1999.

Malone, Peter, ed. *Discovering an Australian Theology*. Homebush, NSW: St. Paul, 1988.

Martin, David. *Pentecostalism: The World Their Parish*. Oxford: Blackwell, 2002.

Massey, Richard. "Response to Rethinking Spirit Baptism by Walter J. Hollenweger." In *Pentecostals after a Century*, edited by Allan H. Anderson and Walter J. Hollenweger, 173–75. Sheffield: Sheffield Academic, 1999.

McClung, L. Grant, Jr. "Pentecostal/Charismatic Perspectives on a Missiology for the Twenty-First Century." *Pneuma* 16 (1994) 1–21.

———. "'Try to Get People Saved': Revisiting the Paradigm of an Urgent Pentecostal Missiology." In *The Globalization of Pentecostalism: A Religion Made to Travel*, edited by Murray W. Dempster et al., 30–51. Carlisle, UK: Regnum, 1999.

McIntyre, John. *The Shape of Pneumatology: Studies in the Doctrine of the Holy Spirit*. London: T. & T. Clark, 1997.

Melba P. Maggay. "Theology, Context and the Filipino Church." In *Communicating Cross-Culturally: Towards a New Context for Missions in the Philippines*, edited by Melba P. Maggay, 55–61. Quezon City, Philippines: New Day, 1989.

Menzies, Robert P. *Empowered for Witness: The Spirit in Luke-Acts*. Sheffield: Sheffield Academic, 1991.

———. "Luke and the Spirit: A Reply to James D. G. Dunn." *Journal of Pentecostal Theology* 4 (1994) 115–38.

Menzies, William W. *Anointed to Serve: The Story of the Assemblies of God*. Vol. 1. Springfield, MO: Gospel, 1971.

Menzies, William W., and Robert P. Menzies. *Spirit and Power: Foundations of Pentecostal Experience*. Grand Rapids: Zondervan, 2000.

Middlemiss, David. *Interpreting Charismatic Experience*. London: SCM, 1996.

Moberg, David O. *The Church as a Social Institution: The Sociology of American Religion*. Englewood Cliffs, NJ: Prentice-Hall, 1962.

Moltmann, Jürgen. *The Trinity and the Kingdom of God*. London: SCM, 1981.

Mulholland, M. Robert. *Invitation to a Journey: A Road Map for Spiritual Formation*. Downers Grove: InterVarsity, 1993.

Mursell, Gordon, ed. *The Story of Christian Spirituality: Two Thousand Years from East to West*. Oxford: Lion, 2001.

National Church Life Survey. "Church Life Resources Workbench." *Australian Spirituality and Religious Beliefs*, 2003. http://www.ncls.org.au/pages.asp?page=121&sao=4.

Bibliography

———. *Winds of Change: The Experience of Church in a Changing Australia*. Edited by Peter Kaldor et al. Homebush West, NSW: Anzea, 1994.

Nida, Eugene A. *Message and Mission: The Communication of the Christian Faith*. Rev. ed. Pasadena, CA: William Carey, 1990.

Nile, Richard. "Civilisation." In *The Australian Legend and Its Discontents: Australian Studies Reader*, edited by Richard Nile, 42–58. St. Lucia: University of Queensland Press, 2000.

O' Dea, Thomas F. "Five Dilemmas of the Institutionalization of Religion." *Journal for the Scientific Study of Religion* 1 (1961) 30–41.

Olson, Bruce E. *Bruchko*. Carol Stream, IL: Creation House, 1973.

Osiek, Carolyn. *What Are They Saying about the Social Setting of the New Testament?* Rev. ed. New York: Paulist, 1992.

Patton, Michael Quinn. *Practical Evaluation*. London: Sage, 1982.

Pew Forum on Religion and Public Life. *Global Christianity: A Report on the Size and Distribution of the World's Christian Population*. December 19, 2011.

Piggin, Stuart. *Evangelical Christianity in Australia: Spirit, Word and World*. Melbourne: Oxford University Press, 1996.

Pinnock, Clark H. "Church in the Power of the Holy Spirit: The Promise of Pentecostal Ecclesiology." *Journal of Pentecostal Theology* 14 (2006) 147–65.

———. *Flame of Love: A Theology of the Holy Spirit*. Downers Grove: InterVarsity, 1996.

Poloma, Margaret M. *The Assemblies of God at the Crossroads: Charisma and Institutional Dilemmas*. Knoxville: University of Tennessee Press, 1989.

Prior, Randall, ed. *The Gospel and Cultures. Initial Explorations in the Australian Context*. Melbourne: Victorian Council of Churches, 1997.

Pritchard, Shiela. "Wells or Fences? The Risk of Spiritual Growth." *Reality*, Feb/Mar 1994, 21–25.

Quebedeaux, Richard. *The New Charismatics II*. San Francisco: Harper & Row, 1983.

Rait, Jill, et al., eds. *Christian Spirituality: High Middle Ages and Reformation*. London: SCM, 1988.

Reiher, Jim. "Women's Participation in Victorian AOG Church Leadership." *Australasian Pentecostal Studies* 7 (2003) 3–34.

Riches, Tanya, and Tom Wagner. "The Evolution of Hillsong Music: From Australian Pentecostal Congregation into Global Brand." *Australian Journal of Communication* 39 (2012) 17–36. www.academia.edu/1910385/The evolution_of_Hillsong_Music_From_Australian_Pentecostal_congregation_into_Global_Brand.

Robertson, Roland. *Globalization: Social Theory and Global Culture*. London: Sage, 1992.

Robinson, Martin. *The Faith of the Unbeliever: Building Innovative Relationships with the Unchurched*. Crowborough, UK: Monarch, 1997.

———. "Response to Critical Issues for Pentecostals by Walter J. Hollenweger." In *Pentecostals after a Century: Global Perspectives on a Movement in Transition*, edited by Allan H. Anderson and Walter J. Hollenweger, 192–96. Sheffield: Sheffield Academic, 1999.

Roebuck, Cecil M., Jr. *The Azusa Street Mission and Revival: The Birth of the Global Pentecostal Movement*. Nashville: Nelson, 2006.

———. "An Emerging Magisterium? The Case of the Assemblies of God." *Pneuma: Journal for the Society for Pentecostal Studies* 25 (2003) 164–215.

———. "Taking Stock of Pentecostalism: The Personal Reflections of a Retiring Editor." *Pneuma: Journal for the Society for Pentecostal Studies* 15 (1993) 39.

Bibliography

Rosenau, Pauline Marie. *Post-Modernism and the Social Sciences: Insights, Inroads and Intrusions*. Princeton: Princeton University Press, 1992.

Saad, Lydia. "Churchgoing Among U.S. Catholics Slides to Tie Protestants." *Gallup*, April 9, 2009. http://www.gallup.com/poll/117382/church-going-among-catholics-slides-tie-protestants.aspx.

Schreiter, Robert. *Constructing Local Theologies*. Maryknoll: Orbis, 1999.

Schwarz, Christian A. *Natural Church Development: A Guide to Eight Essential Qualities of Healthy Churches*. Emmelsbüll, Germany: C&P, 1996.

———. *Paradigm Shift in the Church: How Natural Church Development can Tranform Theological Thinking*. Carol Stream, IL: Church Smart Resources, 1999.

———. *The Threefold Art of Experiencing God: The Liberating Power of a Trinitarian Faith*. Brighton, Queensland: Direction Ministry, 1999.

Schweitzer, E. "Pneuma, Pneumatikos in O.T." In *Theological Dictionary of the New Testament*, edited by Gerhard Kittel and Gerhard Friedrich, 6:396–455. Grand Rapids: Eerdmans, 1968.

Senn, Frank C., ed. *Protestant Spiritual Traditions*. New York: Paulist, 1986.

Sheldrake, Philip. *Spirituality and History*. London: SPCK, 1991.

Shelton, J. B. "A Reply to James D. G. Dunn's Baptism in the Spirit: A Response to Pentecostal Scholarship in Luke-Acts." *Journal of Pentecostal Theology* 4 (1994) 139–43.

Silverman, David, ed. *Qualitative Research: Theory Method and Practice*. London: Sage, 1997.

Singleton, A., et al. "Spirituality in Adolescence and Young Adulthood: A Method for a Qualitative Study." Unpublished paper for Youth Spirituality Reference Group, Melbourne, 2004.

Smith, D., and Smith G. *A River Is Flowing: A History of the Assemblies of God in Australia*. Adelaide: Assemblies of God in Australia Commonwealth Conference, 1987.

Søgaard, Viggo. *Research in Church and Mission*. Pasadena, CA: William Carey, 1996.

Spittler Russell P. "Spirituality, Pentecostal and Charismatic." In *The New International Dictionary of Pentecostal and Charismatic Movements*, edited by S. M. Burgess and E. M. Van Der Maas, 1096–102. Rev. ed. Grand Rapids: Zondervan, 2002.

———. "Suggested Areas for Further Research in Pentecostalism." *Pneuma: Journal of the Society for Pentecostal Studies* 5 (1983) 39.

———. "Theological Style among Pentecostals and Charismatics." In *Doing Theology in Today's World*, edited by John D. Woodbridge and Thomas Edward McComiskey, 297. Grand Rapids: Zondervan, 1991.

Stackhouse, John G. "In the World But . . ." *Christianity Today* 46 (2002) 80.

Stark, R., and R. Finke. *Acts of Faith: Explaining the Human Side of Religion*. Berkeley: University of California Press, 2000.

Stockton, Eugene D. *Landmarks: A Spiritual Search in a Southern Land*. Eastwood, NSW: Parish Ministry, 1990.

Stronstad, Roger. *Charismatic Theology of St. Luke*. Peabody: Hendrickson, 1984.

———. *Spirit, Scripture and Theology: A Pentecostal Perspective*. Baguio City, Philippines: Asia Pacific Theological Seminary, 1984.

Synan, Vinson. *The Century of the Holy Spirit: 100 Years of Pentecostal and Charismatic Renewal 1901–2001*. Nashville: Nelson, 2001.

———. *The Holiness Pentecostal Tradition: Charismatic Movements in the 20th Century*. 2nd ed. Grand Rapids: Eerdmans, 1997.

Bibliography

———. "The Origins of the Pentecostal Movement." Holy Spirit Research Center, Oral Roberts University Library, Tulsa, Oklahoma. 2002. http://www.oru.edu/ university/ library/holyspirit/pentorg1.html.

———. "The Pentecostal 20th Century." *Ministries Today*, Nov.Dec. 1999, 26–35.

———. "The Role of Tongues as Initial Evidence." In *Spirit and Renewal: Essays in Honour of J. Rodman Williams*, edited by Mark W. Wilson, 69–82. Sheffield: Sheffield Academic, 1994.

Taylor, John V. *The Go-Between God: The Holy Spirit and the Christian Mission*. London: SCM, 1972.

Thompson, M. J. *Soul Feast: An Invitation to the Christian Spiritual Life*. Louisville: Westminster John Knox, 1995.

Tidball, Derek. *An Introduction to the Sociology of the New Testament*. Exeter, Devon: Paternoster, 1983.

———. *The Social Context of the New Testament*. Reprint. Carlisle, UK: Paternoster, 1997.

Tippet, Alan R. *Introduction to Missiology*. Pasadena, CA: William Carey, 1987.

Toon, Peter. *What Is Spirituality and Is It for Me?* London: Daybreak, 1989.

VandeCreek, Larry, et al. *Research in Pastoral Care and Counselling: Quantitative and Qualitative Approaches*. Decatur, GA: Journal of Pastoral Care Publications, 1994.

Villafañe, Elfin. *The Liberating Spirit*. Grand Rapids: Eerdmans, 1994.

Volf, Miroslav. *After Our Likeness: The Church as the Image of the Trinity*. Grand Rapids: Eerdmans, 1988.

———. *Wir sind die Kirche*. Tubingen: Habilitationschrift, 1992.

Wakefield, Gordon S., ed. *Dictionary of Christian Spirituality*. London: SCM, 1990.

Webb, William J. *Slaves, Women and Homosexuals: Exploring the Hermeneutics of Cultural Analysis*. Downers Grove: InterVarsity, 2001.

Weber, Max. *Basic Concepts in Sociology*. Translated and introduced by H. P. Secher. London: Owen, 1962.

———. *The Sociology of Religion*. Boston: Beacon, 1963. Reprint, 1991.

———. *The Theory of Social and Economic Organization*. New York: Free, 1947.

Wenk, Matthias. "The Holy Spirit as Transforming Power within a Society: Pneumatological Spirituality and Its Political/Social Relevance for Western Europe." *Journal of Pentecostal Theology* 11 (2002) 130–42.

Westwood, Christine. "The Psalm Remains the Same." *Australian*, 4 May 2004.

Whittaker, Colin. *Korea Miracle: The Extraordinary True Story of Yonggi Cho and the Korean Miracle*. Eastbourne, UK: Kingsway, 1988.

Whyte, William Foote, ed. *Participatory Action Research*. London: Sage, 1991.

Williams, J. Rodman. "Harvey Cox and Pentecostalism: A Review of Fire From Heaven." *Australasian Pentecostal Studies* 1 (1998) 23–26.

———. *Renewal Theology: Systematic Theology from a Charismatic Perspective*. Grand Rapids: Zondervan, 1996.

Wilson, Bruce. *Can God Survive Australia?* Sutherland, NSW: Albatross, 1983.

Wilson, Everett A. "They Crossed the Red Sea, Didn't They? Critical History and Pentecostal Beginnings." In *The Globalization of Pentecostalism: A Religion Made to Travel*, edited by Murray W. Dempster et al, 85–115. Carlisle, UK: Regnum, 1999.

Winter, Ralph D., and Steven C. Hawthorne, eds. *Perspectives on the World Christian Movement: A Reader*. 3rd ed. Pasadena: William Carey, 1999.

Wolffe, John, ed. *Global Religious Movements in Regional Context*. Religion Today: Tradition, Modernity and Change 4. Aldershot, UK: Ashgate, 2002.

Bibliography

Yong, Amos. *Discerning the Spirit(s): A Pentecostal- Charismatic Contribution to Christian Theology of Religions.* Edited by J. C. Thomas et al. Journal of Pentecostal Theology Supplement Series 20. Sheffield: Sheffield Academic, 2000.

Young, Frances M. *The Theology of the Pastoral Epistles.* Cambridge: Cambridge University Press, 1994.

Zikmund, Barbara Brown, et al. *Clergy Women: An Uphill Calling.* 1st ed. Louisville: Westminster John Knox, 1998.

www.ingramcontent.com/pod-product-compliance
Lightning Source LLC
Chambersburg PA
CBHW072148160426
43197CB00012B/2293